SURVIVING
GLOBAL
SLAVERY

LIVING UNDER THE NEW
WORLD ORDER

by

Robert K. Spear

Dedicated to those who will have to face the Tribulations. May this help them survive!

Designer, typesetting, editing, and illustrations: Robert K. Spear

Cover design: Carrie Hanes

UNIVERSAL FORCE DYNAMICS

P.O. Box 410
Leavenworth, KS 66048
(913) 682-6518

Orders: (800) 368-0877
TREK-800, Dept. UFD
P.O. Box I
Cave Junction, OR 97523

ISBN: 0-9622627-8-1

Library of Congress Number:

DISCLAIMER

ABOUT UFD & THE AUTHOR

Universal Force Dynamics (UFD) Publishing got its name from a set of conflict management theories developed by Robert K. Spear from the Eastern martial arts and Western military and business science. These theories have been used by the Army's Command and General Staff College to develop new tactics. The Dallas Cowboys football team has used them to teach movement to new linemen. The principles of UFD figure prominently in several of Bob's personal security books.

UFD is located in Leavenworth, Kansas, near the U.S. Army's Command and General Staff College and Combined Arms Command. It has been in business since 1989. Co-located with it is Bob's retail bookstore, The Book Barn, in business since 1979. It is run by Bob's wife, Barb. Editorial questions should be directed there. Order fulfillment is accomplished in Cave Junction, OR, by TREK-800.

Robert K. Spear is a man of many accomplishments. A 6th degree black belt, he is considered an American pioneer in the Korean scientific street fighting art, Hapkido (the way of coordinated power). The first American to attain a 3rd degree black belt and instructor's certification in Korea, back in 1975, Bob is currently the Chairman of the Board of Examiners for the U.S. Hapkido Federation. Bob has written and presented numerous academic papers on the martial arts and is internationally recognized as a martial arts theorist and author. He has presented trainings on three continents to general military, special operations, Military Intelligence, security forces, and civilian personnel, since 1974.

Raised on a self-sufficient farm in Indiana, Bob writes articles for several survivalist and martial art magazines. He spent 25 years in Military Intelligence and deception operations. He holds BS degrees in both Music and Business from Indiana University (he used to play guitar and arrange music for the Tommy Dorsey Orchestra and was a professional band player and studio musician for six years) and an MS in Business from the University of Northern Colorado.

iii

TABLE OF CONTENTS

vi

FOREWORD

During the Desert Shield/Desert Storm conflict, President George Bush began using the words, **"A New World Order"**. Every time I heard them my hackles rose, but I didn't know why. A professional military intelligence specialist by trade, I tend to look for hidden meanings in most things around me. My good wife, Barbara, calls me a professional paranoid. My natural response was to head for the excellent library at the U.S. Army's Command and General Staff College at Ft. Leavenworth, Kansas. This was followed by a trip to our municipal library to use their computerized links into national research data bases. I quickly saw references to a book I had read years before called [1]**"None Dare Call It Conspiracy"** by Gary Allen. Upon rereading it, much started to click into place for me. Several magazine and journal articles reenforced my fears.

These sources all pointed toward a conspiracy of extremely wealthy power brokers throughout the world who have been seeking for decades, nay, centuries, to form an overarching world government which allowed them total dominion over all mankind— a dominion which would result in the framework for rule by the Anti-Christ AND IS

SATANIC IN ORIGIN.

I know what you probably are saying. "Yes, Mr. Spear, you really are paranoid. Imagine someone being able to do such a thing! This is crazy!"

Looking at it from a distance, I might be inclined to agree with you; however, much better men than I also came up with similar findings and have produced two excellent books on the subject: Pat Robertson's excellent overview, [2]"**The New World Order**" and Gary H. Kah's superbly detailed [3]"**En route to Global Occupation**".

At this point, I must assume my reader has also experienced a few feelings of trepidation or he or she wouldn't have even picked up this book. Rather than wasting half this book's space making a case for a global government threat, I will only briefly describe its structure and goals in Chapter 1. The rest of this book will devote a chapter each to a number of societal areas, such as education, religion, medical considerations, economic concerns, food and water, shelter, etc. In each chapter, I will address the new structure and/or policies as I perceive them. These will be followed by an assessment of their impacts on the lives of good people like yourselves.

Not all is bad news, however. For each impact, I will suggest at least one or more common sense strategies which one may begin working on immediately. The key to this approach is that if I (and others) am wrong in my fears or analysis, you will not be injured by these strategies. In every case, those following these ideas will find they lead to an enriched spiritual and physical life. Even if there is no period of travail and tribulation in our life times, many of these strategies will preserve us if we lose our job unexpectedly or stumble on life's path in some other way. They will even protect us in times of natural disaster. If the future does contain these challenges, you should begin preparation now. Don't wait for them to happen, for it will be too late then! **DO IT NOW!**

This book is written for practicing Christians of all denominations and doctrines. It is also applicable for those non-Christians who believe there may be bad times in the offing. I'm not saying your religion or philosophy is right or wrong. I <u>am</u> suggesting you should leave yourself open to all options and prepare for the worst. It doesn't matter if you believe in a pre-tribulation rapture, a mid-tribulation, or a post-tribulation rapture. We all may experience at least the lead into the times of travail. Again, it can't hurt to be ready for the worst and be pleasantly surprized by the best. We will examine these concepts further throughout the chapters.

I have been personally practicing several of these strategies since 1976 as part of my Church's family preparedness program. Others come from my experiences while growing up on a God-fearing, self-sufficient farm in Northern Indiana. This was during a time my Grandfather transitioned from horse to tractor farming, immediately following World War II. I have shared some of them with the readers of my articles in the [4] **American Survival Guide**, in [5] **Practical Survival Magazine**, and in [6] **Journal for Self Reliant Living**. Now they're yours to use.

The best information resources we know are listed throughout this book. If you can't locate the ones you want at your local bookstore or library, use our handy order blank on the last page.

1. **None Dare Call It Conspiracy** by Gary Allen, Concord Press, 1971 (Out of Print).

2. **The New World Order** by Pat Robertson, Word Publishing, 1991, $16.99 hardback.

3. **En Route To Global Occupation** by Gary H. Kah, Hunnington House Publishers, 1991, $7.95 paperback.

4. **American Survival Guide**, 2145 West La Palma Ave, Anaheim, CA 92825-0015, $26.95 for 12 issues.

5. **Practical Survival Magazine**, Mountain Star Int., 1750 30th St. Suite 496, 1-800-800-7630, $18.00 for 6 issues.

6. **Journal for Self Reliant Living**, Box 910, Merlin, OR 97532, (503) 479-6699, $72.00 for 12 issues.

CHAPTER 1
THE NEW WORLD ORDER

Universal world peace, efficient centralized banking, social programs to support every want, public pre-school for three and four-year-olds, world-wide consumer markets, a wonderfully vivid religion which allows us to achieve our true potential and experience mind-blowingly powerful spiritual experiences, an end to the drug problem, a lessening of street crime and violence, villages networking globally to assist one another in solving administration problems— it all sounds wonderful doesn't it. But, at what price?

These are all benefits touted by globalists, futurists, and New Agers. All these things and much more would come to be if only Man would band together into a one world-wide supernation. What we call countries or nations would become states of this vast overarching monolith.

Back in the early 80's, I used to attend New Age meetings. I even spoke at International World Future Society conventions. I have spoken personally with Marilyn Fergusson, author of the [1]

1

Surviving Global Slavery

Aquarian Conspiracy. I spent several evenings at Barbara Marx Hubbard's Washington, D.C. mansion with highly placed global activists. I attended the Pacific Institute's New Age Leadership Symposium. This was all done in support of my activities with a U.S. Army think tank called Task Force Delta while I worked as a civil servant at Ft. Leavenworth, Kansas. These activities were funded by the Army and were considered part of my duties. It wasn't until later on, in the 1990's, I learned who was behind these agendas and what their true goals were.

One might ask if I regretted my role in all this. I would have to say no. It is because of these experiences that I know the enemy for what and who they are. This personal exposure has made me much more discerning.

Lethal Control

The true issue here is control of peoples' lives throughout the world. Control by deception or by coercion— whatever it takes. If one is a member of a non-productive group or a dissenting body, ways will be found to eliminate any bothersomeness one might produce. This might be at pain of death. Numbers aren't a problem.

The Global 2000 study, commissioned by President Jimmy Carter, predicted by the turn of this century, the Southern Hemisphere have-nots would be so numerous and so desperate, they would probably attempt to overthrow the Northern Hemisphere countries. This threat is no longer

The New World Order

as great. Look at the death rates in India. Withholding food makes a marvelously cheap strategic weapon. Watch for similar control means being used in the various Russian Commonwealth republics and Central Europe.

In early 1992, we see 60+% of Africa's adult population infected with the AIDS virus. A significant portion of African children are now orphans, or soon will be. How fortuitous that so many valuable natural resources will become available when all these bothersome savages die off.

In U.S. urban ghettos, drug users share needles. Why? Because needles were made illegal and are, therefore, difficult to obtain. They were made illegal when it was first noted that AIDS could be spread by the sharing of needles. Inner-city AIDS rates are skyrocketing. Ghettos are predicted to become ghost towns by the year 2000.

Yes, the bottom line is control of people by whatever means necessary. Those people behind the scenes who have been pushing for total global control will stop at nothing. Their ruthlessness stems not only from their lust for personal power and greed for material riches beyond imagination, but from Satanic inspired advisors and helpmates.

The New Age Connection

There are any number of books which have been written to expose the New Age Movement's links with Satan's occultic kingdom. The two best books I have found to explain this oft-confusing, highly complex quasi-religion/philosophy set are: [2] **The New Age Messiah** by Troy Lawrence, and [3] **Inside the New Age Nightmare** by Randall N. Baer. Both are written by individuals who were high up enough in its organization (before they were born again in the Lord) to know its **true** aims and intents.

Basically the New Agers would have us believe that all things are possible because God is within us. In fact, they say, God **is** us! He is also the Universe, and the trees, whales, rocks, and some swami living in a Pakistani tenement in Soho, London. All their focus is upon Self and self-improvement. There is no room for redemption, faith, and good works. Every piece of additional knowledge toward better self development comes with a price tag. There is no free lunch and no true caring for others beyond recruitment into the next "Way" or "Path".

New Age consultants have been making huge amounts of money training and guiding the highest levels of government and industrial leaders and administrators since at least the late 1970's. One old acquaintance of mine made quite a name for himself in government circles teaching neuro linguistic programing to General officers and Congressional representatives while he was on active Army duty.

This extremely powerful methodology comes from the psych and counseling field. It has been used by skilled practitioners to track a person's brain activity by observing eye movement and body language. Once the brain activity has been identified, certain insidious, subtle techniques are used to gain the subject's trust and to actually interfere and change thought processes and attitudes. This has been successfully used by U. S. Army prisoner of war interrogators since 1983. Can you imagine the power this might place at the disposal of a government leader or a captain of industry? Are you willing to trust they would use these skills in an ethical manner? My friend became so well known for teaching these skills to the select few, he turned down a promotion to full Colonel so he could retire and continue this work as a private corporate consultant.

Another acquaintance of mine makes $15,000+ a weekend plus expenses by going to Fortune 100 company Directors' strategist meetings. He guides them through a global transformational process, helping them to set goals and objectives for the next 10-20 years. He captures these visually on butcher paper hung all over the room. After the meeting, he goes home to a beautiful tropical getaway on the big island of Hawaii. There, he and his staff produce lovely professional slides of this visual roadmap of the future.

"So what's wrong with that?", you might ask. It so happens that before he retired from the Army's military intelligence corps, he became its leading expert on the New Age movement and even developed a military model of it to use as a training media for his fellow officers and many other acquaintances. When he retired from the service, he had personally experienced over 140 New Age trainings— from Rolfing to EST to meditation to spoon bending, and so on. He uses a conglomeration of many of these techniques and methodologies from the occult to train and guide corporate leaders at the highest levels.

This type of advising has given rise to a whole new field of study in our business schools called Transformational Change Facilitation. This grew out of a related topical area called Organizational Development or Organizational Effectiveness. The problem is in the end result of the transformation. It may result in a kinder and gentler organization, but one which is guided by occultic principles.

The scary aspect of these occultic influences and globalist agendas is the pervasiveness and insidiousness of their introduction to society in general. Many, like myself, really didn't understand the basic evilness of their origins and their inherent dangers. I practiced several of the more dangerous methodologies for years without becoming aware of the spiritual risks I was taking. But, more on that in Chapter 6. It is amazing how these agendas and their advocates keep popping up in the most dangerous of places. The following is a true story which happened to me in December of 1991.

The New World Order

A Frightening Encounter With the New World Order

When I was selected to attend a U.S. Army training course called, "Personnel Management for Executives", I welcomed the two-week stay in the Overland Park, Kansas, Marriott hotel as a respite. My normal work routine includes my full-time position as a civil servant (euphemism for bureaucrat), running my small publishing company, assisting my wife with her duties at our bookstore, staying actively involved with church work, and squeezing some quality time in with my family. This short training experience was designed to get almost seventy GM-13 through 15s and a few military officers away from their work environment and daily cares. It would give us a chance to recharge our batteries listening to live presentations and videos of some of the country's better business and management speakers.

The goal of this extended workshop was to provide selected mid-level managers in our service the latest tools, concepts, and trends in managing the Federal work force. My class mates were all highly experienced government administrators from a wide variety of Army activities and agencies scattered throughout the Midwest and West.

It was the second to the last day of the session. The course administrators had provided excellent speakers throughout the two-week period, but they were especially excited about today's guest. I had read his biographical sketch and listened with interest to his introduction by one of the course leaders.

"Dr. Nicholas Goncharoff is an educator and specialist in the fields of politics, science, comparative history, management, and international affairs. After fighting for his native Russia as a young officer in World War II, Dr. Goncharoff joined relatives of his prominent Kiev family in Munich, Germany, to obtain a doctorate in History and Philosophy. He has done post-doctoral work at Cambridge and at Columbia Universities. He has spoken at over 600 colleges and universities throughout the United States, Canada, Europe, and Asia. He also founded the North-American YMCA Statesmanship Program which takes outstanding community leaders from the U.S. and Canada to various parts of the world, exposing them to prominent international decision makers and destiny molders. He is frequently asked to serve as an advisor and consultant in matters of foreign trade by corporations and governments. Just this week Russian leader, Boris Yeltsin, invited Dr. Goncharoff to be his U.S./Canada Trade Advisor."

During the thunderous welcoming applause, I thought to myself. "Man, is this guy ever connected! This talk should really be interesting!" In addition, his physical presence was impressive. Dressed in an expensive light grey "Bankers" suit, his leonine silver hair and quaint Euro-Russian accent reeked of validity.

The New World Order

What followed, however, left me literally shaking and nauseated. I've been around the intelligence business for a fairly long time— since 1967. During my career, I've had the opportunity to meet some pretty smooth operators. This guy beat them all hands down. I have never seen a better propagandist. What made his presentation especially dangerous was the setting of the training. We had been separated from our day-to-day realities for two weeks. We had been asked to listen to the speakers with an open mind. All our lectures had dealt with the fact that enormous changes were taking place in the world and within our organizations and we needed to prepare for them. For those readers who have had some POW or psychological warfare training you will recognize this environment as being ideal for classical "Brain Washing". The class and its administrators were being programmed and they didn't even know it.

As the lecture progressed, I counted only four of us who perceived what was happening and understood how disturbing the message was. The rest of the attendees were enthralled with this extremely urbane Russian's patter. They were almost in love with the guy and were accepting everything he said as if it was the sermon on the mount. Afterwards they gushed profusely over his words and him.

Throughout the lecture I took notes madly and was able to question him in an encouraging manner during the breaks and the lecture to elicit as much as I could about where he was coming from. For those readers who understand the background of globalist government theory and organization, Dr. Goncharoff freely admitted to having worked on the Council on Foreign Relations— that august body funded by the likes of the Rockefellers and other Tri-Lateralist string pullers, which has advised all our presidents since the late sixties.

I have seen the enemy and he is scary. Herein follows the essence of what this highly effective globalist change agent had to say. Notice the interesting mixture of secular humanism, New Age, and socialistic concepts couched in modern management terms and combined with very noble sounding concepts. Understand also how attractive this presentation was to an audience of experienced government administrators— individuals who have raised their hands to swear to uphold the constitution against all enemies, foreign or domestic. His lecture addressed many of the geopolitical events and changes currently taking place. My comments are in parenthesis and italics:

The Need For Language Training

"The wave of the future is upon us right now. We are witnessing the rapid dissolution of nationalistic barriers. Now, more than ever, you must learn to speak the languages of our global community if you want to help or compete in this environment. Every one of you should spend the next three years studying another language. I speak five Euro-Russian languages and am currently studying Mandarin Chinese. Language training should start in our pre-schools. *(This supports the National Education Association's goal of mandatory schooling from three-years-old on).* You should learn Russian, an Asian language, and Spanish since it will soon be the tongue spoken by the soon-to-be new ethnic majority in the United States."

(I have no problem with language learning. It is a valuable asset for understanding what is going on in the world and can help us interface with others. What is scary is the developing demographics of language mix and where the changes are taking place, ie.,the U.S.).

Global Economics

"The conversion to the European Economic Community is rapidly moving forward. Within the next week or so, they are expected to come to an agreement on a common monetary unit with a conversion rate for all parties concerned. **With the developments in the Russian Commonwealth of republics, I believe the European Economic Community should be extended from the Atlantic across Europe to the Pacific.** We are moving from military to economic superpowers. Japan and Germany have already accomplished monetarily much of what they set out to do militarily."

"One of the greatest dangers in the world today is America's shaky banking situation. *(I'm glad he recognizes this fact!)* We can fix this by taking a global viewpoint. Within one to five years, we should be ready for a common world-wide economic unit." *(This means doing away with the dollar as we know it. There will be only one world-wide currency. I asked Dr. Goncharoff during a break when the world would be able to go to a cashless monetary system, one run by computers. He down-played this possibility, saying this would be so complex it would not happen until the end of the next century. Actually, the hardest part of converting to a centrally controlled cashless society is the agreement on a common economic unit. The computer technology infrastructure is do-able from off-the-shelf capabilities right now. His 1-5 year prediction scares the heck out of me).*

New World Politics and Needs

"As your military downsizes, some of your jobs may be abolished. Your skills, however, are desperately needed in the Russian Commonwealth. We need your understanding of Western management systems applied to government. Boris Yeltsin told me last week he needs the following skills from the Americans:

- Specialists in the global economic system
- Teachers of entrepreneurism
- Foreign languages
- U.S. Army Corps of Engineers and related civil engineering specialists
- Managerial force and middle-management trainers
- Agriculture production trainers
- Trainers of how to capitalize on women-power"

The New World Order

(Wow, talk about technology transfer. What makes this treasonous is his use of a realistic threat, the loss of government worker jobs, with the carrot of coming to Russia to teach them how to do it. I know this will bother readers who don't believe the communist threat is over. I find it even more insidious in that the globalists are actively recruiting so-called constitution defending Americans to play a role in a great leveling or equalization process which insures across the board socialist equalization of the U.S. and Russia. If all nation states become equal in how they do internal business, it becomes much easier to control them. He then said:

"Stabilization is the key *(don't rock the boat)*. Global control of the spread of nuclear weapons is essential. A consolidation of the Northern hemisphere will help make this happen. There are no more conservatives or liberals, only closed minds and open minds. The greatest threat to the world are the fundamentalist Islamics."

(When asked what he thought of Pat Buchannon, he said he believed the republicans were offering Buchannon as a counter-balance to David Duke. Their platforms are similar but Buchannon doesn't have the KKK/Neo Nazi stigma). It was also interesting that Dr. Goncharoff believed Buchannon probably didn't personally believe all that he espoused. I got the impression he was saying Pat Buchannon was a token conservative Uncle Tom and controlled by the Globalist movement. He never said this directly, but I inferred it

Surviving Global Slavery

from the way he spoke about the man.

Managerial Education

"Who is our enemy? We ourselves are! We must get involved in our education system. It needs revamping *(he never detailed how)*. We must customize our managerial education system to the needs of the second and third world clients. We need to reject traditional academic centers of education since they have become too bogged down with "publish or perish" and other bureaucratic requirements. We need to develop business and government funded managerial universities based on the global view. The same would provide a School of Statesmanship education for our politicians. The U.S. needs to take this leadership role. **The U.S. military/industrial complex will find jobs in this international role.** Unselfish love is the ultimate goal of management. **Reeducation** will fulfill this current spiritual emptiness within management. Management should provide three things:

 • Control and direct leadership and management with vision
 • Kindness and objective firmness
 • Treat people with judgement and love, but with long-range flexibility."

(What unmitigated high-minded crap Note the operant words: control, firmness, judgement, long-range flexibility. This sounds like "1984 Newspeak" to me.)

Future of Religion

The New World Order

"Most of mankind's bloodiest wars were fought in the name of religion. I believe we should place a moratorium on all religions for 100 years! *(Oh well, there went that freedom!)* Then we should combine the best aspects of all the world religions and management systems as a basis for a new operation system *(read control system here)*. The Old God is obsolete, a new universal God is needed. A new ethics system should be constructed which looks like this:
1. Human relations in toto.
2. Relations between you and me.
3. Our relationship to the planet earth.
4. The relationship between man and his universe.
5. The relationship between us and the Cosmos."

"Enthusiasm translates from Greek into the God within us. This is the wholeness of our development."

(Note, there is no role for God or Christ in this framework! He also implied that fundamentalist Christianity is as dangerous as fundamentalist Islam in his comments.)

Conclusion

Well, there you have it. This is what is being presented to U.S. military government workers. In all fairness to the course administrator, she had invited Dr. Goncharoff because he was purported to be a dynamic speaker and because he had been involved as a trainer of government

Surviving Global Slavery

managers <u>for over ten years</u>. In the meantime, Dr. Goncharoff successfully pulled the wool over 66 out of seventy peoples' eyes in our class. As I mentioned before, this man was the kind people love to love. He really was that good as a change agent for the globalists. I fear for our future!

Global Government Structure

So far we've discussed several happenings in this author's experience which demonstrate common events leading to world dominion by those seeking the New World Order. Lets now examine the structure of this overarching supergovernment which may soon be ruling us. On pages 21-24 are shown its organization as proposed by those who have accepted the responsibility to write its constitution— the World Constitution and Parliament Association. An original copy of this structure and its supporting Constitution for the Federation of the Earth may be had by sending $5.00 to The World Constitution and Parliament Association, 1480 Hoyt St, Suite 31, Lakewood, CO 80215, USA.

Gary Kah's book, [4] **En Route to Global Occupation**, goes into fine detail as to what this new government intends to do and how much it will cost (trillions). I think the most important information the reader should take away from studying this structure is how complex it is, who is being given the power, and how many, many aspects of life will come under its control. There seems to be an administration division or office for

The New World Order

just about everything we could do or have done for us in life. It doesn't matter what you do, some organization is responsible for overwatching it. This is a Liberal's wildest dream— total government involvement in our lives. Is it any wonder why Satan and his minions have been striving so hard to see this come about. Here is the ready made framework for the Anti-Christ to take over. All in the name of Peace and Brotherhood of course.

Earth Worship

One of the central themes of this new government is the driving need to "save the earth". Now I agree mankind has not done well with their stewardship. Genesis 1:26 states, "And God said, *'Let us make man in our image, after our likeness: and let them have dominion over the fish of the sea, and over the fowl of the air, and over the cattle, and over all the earth, and over every creeping thing that creepeth upon the earth.'"* We were expected to watch over these resources and use them to our own benefit.

Mankind has certainly abused its rights over the millennia. Still, nowhere does the Lord say to <u>worship</u> the earth and the things upon it. The New World Order's religion, the New Age Movement, would say otherwise. They would put man's interests and welfare subordinate to the earth and its creatures and natural resources. More than subordination, they would require homage be paid to the earth in a worshipful fash-

17

ion. This teaching subverts the Lord's intention for man to learn to garner his resources while enjoying the fruits of his labor.

By examining the proposed governmental structure following this chapter, we find at least eleven governmental administration organizations dedicated to controlling the earth and its environment. Can you imagine what an incredible mess that could become. Remember, we're talking about eleven separate agencies. Each one of them will be spewing forth regulations and laws. With the follies of the EPA as a model, the amount of life-controlling bureaucratic rules and impositions would be mind-numbing.

The Bottom Line

The case for earth-guarding/worship is just an example. The real name of the game is control of our every moment. Remember, total control (dominion) over the earth's citizens has been Satan's goal since before the Garden of Eden. If we allow the New World Order to come about, we will have opened ourselves up to a life of puppet playing, but we won't hold the strings. This is a battle for more than our minds and bodies, they want our very souls.

The purpose of this book is to help you keep your souls first and foremost, while keeping life and limb together as much as possible until our Savior comes. Only one world government was ever intended— one which is lead by our Lord

18

The New World Order

Jesus for a thousand-year Golden Age. His will be a government of freedom, love, and self-sufficiency for that is the Lord God's plan. Its structure will be much less complex I'm sure. We don't know its details yet, but he'll let us know in his own good time. In the meantime, hang in there brother and sister until he comes to claim his own. The rest of this book is devoted to helping you hang in there. Now lets see how the New World Order advocates and Satan intend to control you and how you can defend yourselves from them. **God bless you and your preparations!**

RESOURCES

The books listed in the resources sections throughout this book are available through our mailorder service. See the order section at the end of this book.

1. **The Aquarian Conspiracy** by Marilyn Fergusson, J.P. Tarcher, 1981, $10.95.

2. **The New Age Messiah** by Troy Lawrence, Huntington House Publishers, 1991, $8.95.

3. **Inside the New Age Nightmare** by Randall N. Baer, Huntington House Publishers, 1989, $7.95.

4. **En Route to Global Occupation** by Gary Kah, Huntington House Publishers, 1991, $8.95.

THE PEOPLE OF THE WORLD

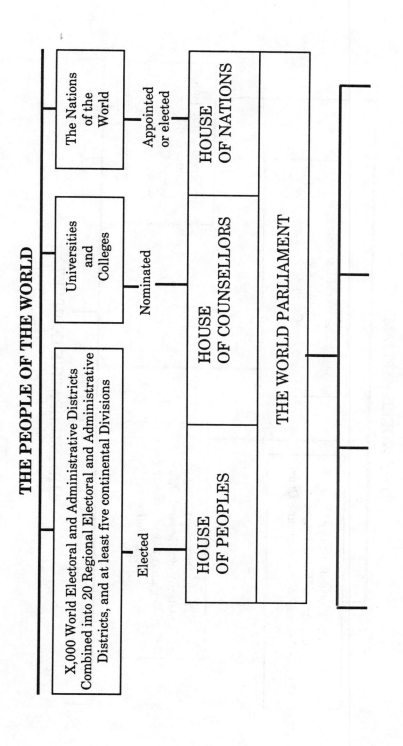

X,000 World Electoral and Administrative Districts Combined into 20 Regional Electoral and Administrative Districts, and at least five continental Divisions

Universities and Colleges

The Nations of the World

Elected

Nominated

Appointed or elected

HOUSE OF PEOPLES

HOUSE OF COUNSELLORS

HOUSE OF NATIONS

THE WORLD PARLIAMENT

THE WORLD PARLIAMENT

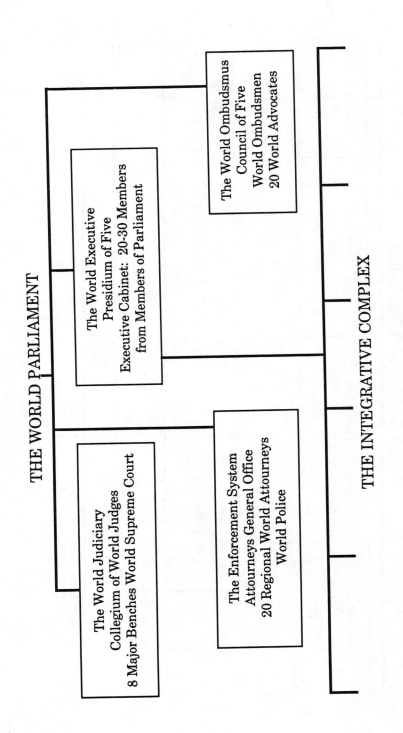

The World Judiciary
Collegium of World Judges
8 Major Benches World Supreme Court

The World Executive
Presidium of Five
Executive Cabinet: 20-30 Members
from Members of Parliament

The World Ombudsmus
Council of Five
World Ombudsmen
20 World Advocates

The Enforcement System
Attourneys General Office
20 Regional World Attourneys
World Police

THE INTEGRATIVE COMPLEX

22

THE INTEGRATIVE COMPLEX

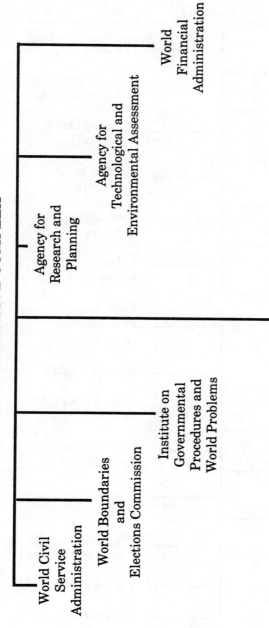

World Civil
Service
Administration

World Boundaries
and
Elections Commission

Institute on
Governmental
Procedures and
World Problems

Agency for
Research and
Planning

Agency for
Technological and
Environmental Assessment

World
Financial
Administration

THE WORLD ADMINISTRATION

THE WORLD ADMINISTRATION

Genetics	The Arts
Education	Communication and Information
Health and Nutrition	Transportation and Travel
Water Supplies and Waterways	Multi-National Corporations
Food and Agriculture	Commerce and Industry
Population	Labor and Income
Disarmament and War Prevention	Economic and Social Development
Habitat and Settlement	Human Rights
Environment and Ecology	Distributive Justice
World Resources	Democratic Procedures
Oceans and Seabeds	World Service Corps
Atmosphere and Space	World Territories Capitols and Parks
Energy	Exterior Relations
Science and Technology	Revenue

CHAPTER 2
COMMERCE
AND
ECONOMICS

Why address economic matters first, one might ask? Because this is what the New World Order will focus on initially to gain dominion over all the peoples of the earth. If you grab the people by their pocket books, their hearts and minds will follow. Some analysts say the New World Order will come in three phases— (1) economic change, (2) political change, and (3) religious change. Although the first chapter presents the political structure, it will be economic controls and manipulations coupled with societal programming which take us into that structure. Once this happens, the population will be ripe for religious change. The key thing to remember is that the New World Order is Satan's plan for world domination. Regardless of what glowing goals and aspirations the globalists and New Agers are proposing, the actual driving force is Satan's need for a control structure of the world's population. To get the spiritual alignment he wants, he will use economics as his primary tool.

25

Surviving Global Slavery

ECONOMICS BASED ON SOCIAL CHANGES

At the time of this book's first draft writing, January, 1992, the European Community had railroaded Great Britain into agreeing to go along with a common EC economic unit of exchange. This is expected to be inaugurated within this year. A precedent is set by this action. Other regions may follow suit out of self-protection. Remember, Dr. Goncharoff predicted the entire world might go to a common economic unit in one to five years. When I queried how long it would be before we went to a cashless society, he tried to allay my concerns by saying that was too hard to do within the next century. He must have had some swamp land to sell me as well. The true challenge is to obtain an agreement on a common economic unit, not the computer technology.

Computerizing all economic transactions is not that difficult. The technology to do so exists today, not a century from now. A gigantic computer complex dedicated to interfacing the world's financial transactions already exists in Belgium. This computer is so large its workers call it "**The Beast**".

I stated before that societal programming would help push us into the New World Order's global government. By this I mean the engineering of social conditions to the point where anarchy, crime, and violence seem to rule. LTC (Ret) Bo

Commerce and Economics

Gritz, America's most highly decorated Special Forces Officer (60+ medals for valor) says in his book, [1] **Called to Serve**, the immense drug trade is fostered and, to a large part, controlled by the CIA. Bo, who spent a career in the so-called "Black Operations" world, says only ten percent of the CIA's covert operations budget comes from Congressional appropriated funds. The other ninety percent comes from drug money, a practice which has gone on since the Vietnam War days. If this is true, it should be no surprise why our country has such a drug problem. The CIA controls it. They give the Drug Enforcement Agency (DEA) just enough leads to make it look like they're making a difference. We Americans are left trying to stuff broken lives back into society. Is it any wonder the public is getting frustrated.

Have you noticed a startling trend related to drugs? Highly organized youth gangs are taking over not just the urban areas, they have moved into small and mid-town USA. Dr. Alan Peterson, an expert on Satanic crime and a national-level police lecturer and trainer on the subject, says that a trend in Satan worship circles is for its leadership to come from the pillars of their communities. Community politicians, police officials, judges, attorneys, doctors, and even ministers are often the secret leaders of covens and Devil-worship groups. Why? For power, money, sex, and all the other rewards the Great Deceiver has always offered. These youth gangs come into a small town, find out who does what to who, offers money under the table to the town fathers (who may also be the leaders of Satanic activity in their town), and sets up business. The ones who are enriched are the same ones involved in secret Satanic combinations.

Inexperienced law enforcement agencies in these towns are hopelessly out-gunned, out-classed, out-maneuvered, and betrayed from the onset. The youth gangs, such as the Bloods or the Crypts, target their recruitment at 12-year-olds and up. Many of their nationwide organizers are in their early 20's; however, they've been in the business for years. They offer a surrogate family to our youth. If a family-vacumn exists, they fill it. What follows is a giant leap in drug related crimes, street violence and murder. As an example, my town, Leavenworth, Kansas, population 37,000, has over 250 members of the Bloods gang. They were organized in November-December 1990. They were supported by areas already well established. In early November, 1990, two van loads of automatic weapons, ammo, and knives were sent to Leavenworth from Wichita, Kansas, a larger town which has been almost taken over by gang activity.

A CASHLESS SOCIETY

Satan has our good citizens on the run. What has all this to do with economics? He has created the societal conditions which will make a cashless society attractive. All the New World Order has to do now is promise to eliminate drug running and stolen-goods fencing by eliminating cash. They will reason that if all financial transactions can be traced and if cash money no longer has value, drug and other crime related financial transactions are doomed. What an attractive enticement that is to dangle before our citizens. Of course, they'll never stop to consider that if you can control the bad guys in this manner, it will also work to control the good guys.

In addition, with all the bank failures and savings and loan scandals, our financial infrastructure is teetering on the brink of total collapse. If it does, the New World Order is prepared to step in to save the day by amalgamating banking control at a worldwide level. In February, 1992, while on a flight from Memphis to Kansas City, I struck up a conversation with the gentleman in the seat next to me. He was a GS-14 (equivalent to someone a little higher in rank than a Lieutenant Colonel) and worked for the Federal Depositors Insurance Corporation. The FDIC is the organization responsible for insuring all our funds after we hand them off to the friendly Federal bank. We were discussing the fact that both of us worked for the government and how hard times seemed to be coming soon. He stated **the only thing holding together the banking community was consummer confidence. If there were to be a run on the banks, our economy will be doomed!** Most of us have known this for years, or at least sensed it. To hear it from one who's job is to safe guard the banking system, however, is especially chilling.

The possibility of a run on our banks became very real this March, 1992, when a bank in the Kansas City suburbs was robbed. The FBI closed its doors for an hour to conduct an investigation. In that short time, people who desired to conduct banking business and finding locked doors panicked. A rumor quickly spread and a run on this bank began and lasted the rest of the day. The Federal Reserve's regional bank and the FDIC had to jump in to reassure customers and bring calm to the situation. Think what would happen if a rumor or a piece of bad news was passed around on a national or international basis.

If the New World Order can create a common economic unit and computerize all financial transactions, they will have the means to bring about a situation foretold in Revelations 13:16-17, King James version:

16. And he causeth all, both small and great, rich and poor, free and bond, to receive a mark (tattoo or imprint, depending on the translation) *in their right hand, or in their foreheads; 17. And that no man might buy or sell, save he that had the mark, or the name of the beast, or the number of his name.*

This is one of those crystal clear prophecies. John the Revelator saw the latter-day society controlled by Satan in this fashion. The technology to insure no one bought or sold without such an identifying mark is already here. It could be something like a bar-code. It wouldn't even have to be visible to the naked eye. It might be an infrared visible tattoo. Although we couldn't see it, a machine's sensor could easily do so.

Another possibility is a computer chip implanted beneath the skin. A good friend of mine, John LeBourgeois, came up with an idea for a cybernetic dog-tag back in the early 1980's. The Army developed it (without recompense to John, I might add). It carried all essential personnel and medical data on one tiny little computer chip which was embedded in a plastic dog tag.

Currently, computer chips have been implanted in animals to track them in the wild, and most recently in Los Angeles, to track stray pets. These chips have been the size of a grain of rice. In the House Arrest program, which was started by communities which have run out of jail space, prisoners have had similar chips affixed to a non-removeable wrist band. To insure they, in fact, stayed at home, their chips were tracked by satelite-based watch dogs. The idea of implanting a computer chip beneath the surface of the skin which allows its bearer to interface into the world-wide financial transaction network is not farfetched at all. The fact that such a chip could also be used to track one's whereabouts from an eye-in-the-sky is especially chilling to me. What a setup for complete societal control. The possibilities make "1984" and "Logan's Run" seem like Sunday School picnics. But don't worry, be happy, the New World Order is going to take care of you! We don't have to worry about drug-crazed criminals and filthy cash anymore. Our banks will never fail again because "we're keeping our eyes on them".

ECONOMIC IMPACTS

What happens to the practicing Christian who accepts this mark, tattoo, or device? Revelations 14:9-11 states:

9. And the third angel followed them, saying with a loud voice, If any man worship the beast and his image, and receive his mark in his forehead, or in his hand, 10. The same shall drink of the wine of the wrath of God, which is poured out without mixture into the cup of his indignation: and he shall be tormented with fire and brimstone in the presence of the Lamb: 11. And the smoke of their torment ascendeth up for ever and ever: and they have no rest day nor night, who worship the beast and his image, and whosoever receiveth the mark of his name.

Oh wow, big time bummer. If we accept the mark, we are literally damned to hell. If we don't accept it, we and our children are going to starve. Without a mark, chip, or whatever, we can't get paid for our work. We can't buy food or medicine. We can't pay our rent, our mortgage, our taxes. No doctor will treat our family. We won't even be able to receive welfare or food stamps. **MOST IMPORTANTLY, THIS PASSAGE INDICATES THERE WILL BE CHRISTIANS STILL AROUND TO ACCEPT OR REJECT THE MARK OF THE BEAST**. This seems to be a clear indicator that the rapture will not have taken place at this time, or that there will be a number of Christians who won't get raptured for whatever reason.

Commerce and Economics

Many of us interpret the parable of the ten virgins in Matthew, Chapter 25 as illustrating the importance of spiritual preparedness. A good case, however, could be made for a meaning of latter day temporal preparedness as well.

Remember, there were ten virgins who had been invited to a wedding feast and were awaiting the arrival of the bridegroom. The five wise virgins had oil on hand for their lamps. The five foolish virgins had forgotten to bring any oil. At midnight, the bridegroom came and the ten virgins awoke to go out to meet him. The foolish five said, "Oh please, let us have some of your oil!" The wise five said, "Sorry, go out and buy your own, we need ours." The foolish five ran out and bought oil. When they got to the wedding feast, however, the bridegroom said, "I know you not," and didn't let them in.

Why wouldn't he recognize them? Was it perhaps because they had to accept the mark of the beast to buy their oil? When they came back, the bridegroom saw the mark and had to say, "I'm sorry, you are no longer identified as one of mine."

Remember, the parable of the Ten Virgins is specifically about the last days. If you haven't been wise, if you haven't stored oil for your lamps (ie. the wherewithal to live through the last days), and if you accept the mark of the beast to provide for your families, you will be damned eternally.

Surviving Global Slavery

A FINITE PERIOD

How long would you be prepared to live on your own resources? How long will you have to? Yeah, I know what all the pre-tribulations advocates are saying. "Oh, we don't have to worry about any of this. We'll be raptured before anything bad happens. God would never let his elect suffer." If that's true, tell it to the Christians facing the lions in the Roman coliseums. God and Christ don't punish Christians like this, Satan does. We have only the interpretations of well-intentioned men to assure us of a pre-tribulation Rapture. What if they're wrong? Would we be failing Christ's test of faith to prepare for the coming bad times? Or, would we be failing man's. Faith in the Lord Jesus is the only test we should be concerned about!

All is not lost, however. The Lord doesn't expect us to have to put up with the Anti-Christ and his New World Order minions too long. Again, Revelations 13 tells us: ...*and power was given unto him to continue forty and two months (* three and a half years).

If we do not accept the mark of the beast, a specific promise has been made in Revelations 14:12-13:

Here is the patience of the saints: here are they that keep the commandments of God, and the faith of Jesus. 13. And I heard a voice from heaven saying unto me, Write, Blessed are the dead which die in the Lord from henceforth: Yea, saith the

34

Commerce and Economics

Spirit, that they may rest from their labours; and their works do follow them.

Again, here is a clear indication that Christians or "saints" will die <u>after</u> the mark of the beast is offered them. This also seems to be an indication there will be no pre-tribulation rapture.

STRATEGIES FOR SURVIVAL

Cash will no longer be acceptable for use. Use of checks, electronic transfers, and plastic bank cards such as VISA or Mastercard will require the mark of the beast. For those of you who reject that mark, the only economic system left is bartering and self-sufficiency. You won't be able to earn a salary then; however, it might be possible to exist by working for goods and services from one another or from those who have accepted the mark.

I will address self sufficiency in Chapter 5. For now let us discuss those resources which will have value for bartering. These could include:

- Food and garden seeds
- Ammunition
- Gas, kerosene, oil
- Vehicle spare parts
- Fire wood
- Commodities such as soap, tooth paste, etc.
- Clothing
- Medical supplies

Surviving Global Slavery

- Books
- Home schooling supplies and resources
- Silver coins from pre-1967
- Skilled and unskilled services/labor

These sound like the things which should be stored for self sufficiency and they are. Not everyone will have everything they should to get through three and a half years of living on their own resources. If you have extra supplies, they may be worth their weight in gold.

FOOD AND GARDEN SEEDS

Staples which are easily stored and condiments such as salt, pepper, spices, sugar, and honey are excellent. Fresh meat, vegetables, and fruit produced beyond your needs, can be used to acquire other things you might need. The garden seeds you store should be non-hybrid, true-reproducing varieties. They may not be as disease and insect resistant, but they are not dependent on petroleum-based fertilizer and will breed true every time. Most of our hybrid strains will produce wonderful plants; however, the seed from that generation will produce strains not so perfect, and sometimes not even usable. See Chapter 5's Resources section for information on heirloom seed companies.

AMMUNITION

It is possible that bullets may be the coinage of a future barter system. Some types are better

Commerce and Economics

than others. I cannot claim to be a firearms expert, my background concentrates on unarmed and armed hand-to-hand combat. However, I've been around enough firearms and have talked with enough firearm experts to have a fair idea of the basics.

You should store a mixture of commonly found calibers and types and a few uncommon ones (which may have higher potential bartering value). Those rounds more commonly found are:

.22 cal
12 gauge shotgun shells with game loads
.38 caliber pistol
9mm pistol
.30-06 caliber rifle
.45 caliber pistol
.357 caliber pistol

Those which are more unusual but will have value are:

.308 caliber rifle (7.62mm NATO round)
.223 caliber rifle (5.56mm NATO round)
10mm pistol
.44 caliber pistol
7mm Mauser rifle
12 gauge shotgun with double ought loads, flechettes, etc.
AK-47 rifle rounds

Notice that many in the second group are assault, combat, and sniper weapon oriented. Some of these are included in the first group as well.

You should plan on stockpiling at least 10,000 rounds of each type round you have chosen to use personally. For bartering, you should additionally store 1,000 - 5,000 rounds of a few of those from the above two lists.

It's possible to order ammunition direct from the factory; however, it's cheaper to buy reloaded and fabricated ammunition from one of the many companies which produce these. I have found the larger gun and knife shows to be an excellent source of this kind of ammo. Be careful to get high quality reloads. Some weapon manufactures suggest not shooting reloaded ammo in their guns. You'll need to know enough about your guns as to why suggestions such as these are made. Glock is an example of one such company. They warn against using non-factory ammo in their hand guns because some of these reloads aren't powerful enough to fully kick back the breach, thus causing jamming. One needs to use a "hotter" or more powerful powder load to insure this doesn't happen.

See this chapter's resource section for the best sources of reloaded/fabricated ammo I know. One is highly recommended by Carl Krupp, publisher of the **Journal for Self-Reliant Living**, and the others I discovered at regional gun and knife shows in the Middle West.

If you have the skill and equipment, you might consider stocking up on raw materiel and loading your own. This would be the cheapest way to do it because you'd be using sweat equity.

GAS, KEROSENE, AND OIL

The military calls this subject petroleum, oil, and lubrication or POL. Large scale storage of POL is a challenge. The greatest problem is water condensation which can deteriorate the quality of gas and kerosene. There are additives, however, which assist with countering this product. I would recommend that you contact your county farmers coop for suggestions on how these items can best be stored in your are (this will vary over different geographical areas and climates so there isn't a universal solution for this). Deisel fuel stores best & longest. Water will condense in it also; however, it can be filtered out. Normal gas can lose its punch over time, deisel won't. Considering the storeability of deisel, you may want to purchase a deisel-powered car or truck and garden tractor.

I would recommend trying to estimate your POL usage over a 3-4 year period under constrained conditions and add a little more for barter purposes.

VEHICLE SPARE PARTS

Spare parts such as car and truck oil, fuel, & air filters, tires, inner tubes, points, plugs, brake shoes, shocks, belts, etc. and bicycle tires, tubes, brake pads, chains, cables, etc., will also be needed over time. Spares for garden implements and even tools would be very valuable.

Surviving Global Slavery

Obviously these could be quite expensive. Those parts which must be new, such as filters and such, can be bought gradually over time. Each time you buy a filter for your vehicle, buy a second. For those parts and tools which could be second hand, shop yard sales and auctions. Sometimes amazing deals can be had.

FIREWOOD

Firewood or wood cutting tools will be valuable bartering items. Wood may become the primary source of heating and cooking fuel. If you have excess wood to your needs or are able to cut wood for others, you will have a major barter offering.

COMMODITIES

Every time you go to the store, buy a few extra commodities such as tooth paste, tooth brushes, toilet paper, and anything else you believe will be scarce and highly sought. Keep these separate from your own home storage as a little bartering store stock. The reason why they should be kept separate is for security. If someone drops by to trade for some tooth paste, you don't want to expose your entire self sufficiency stock pile to satisfy his need. Perhaps it is unChristian to suggest your stockage may be at risk from other Christians; however, why purposely provide a clear temptation. When a man's family survival is threatened, anything could happen. Don't take unnecessary risks with your own.

Commerce and Economics

CLOTHING

Extra clothing and cloth to make clothes are obvious resources which will be needed in a barter environment. Start saving those cast-off clothes the kids have outgrown or which are no longer stylish. Durable work clothes will be especially valuable. Even leather for shoes would be helpful. If you don't have many castaways, haunt the yardsales for a while. It's possible to find real bargains at these.

MEDICAL SUPPLIES

Stock up on aspirin and tylonol, bandages and band-aids, scissors, needles and suture thread, antiseptics, etc. If you have prescriptions for medicines and find you don't always use all of them, buy them anyway for your trading stock pile. My knees are totally shot— the left one has had four operations and has little cartilage left and the right has been rebuilt with a cadaver tendon transplant. I take Indocin to keep the inflammation down in these joints. I'm supposed to take two 12- hour capsules a day. On those days when my knees are feeling better or when I'm not stressing them as much, I may take only one or no capsules. I still buy, however, the full complement of medicine when I normally would and stockpile what I don't use. I may not always have access to this medicine and it may come in handy to have excess on hand. Check with your pharmacist as to the shelf life of your medicines before doing this!

You may find medical supplies very handy

for bartering. Remember, the law of supply and demand applies. Many medical supplies are controlled substances. This makes their acquisition that much more difficult to obtain if you refuse to accept Satan's mark.

BOOKS

The fact that you're reading this book proves the worthiness of books and publications as sources of critical survival information. Your survival library may become a bartering library. In return for access to your books, you might receive food, or more likely, labor. This could work out quite well in the area of food production. By trading labor for information, you can get help in your garden while teaching the information seekers hands-on skills.

A classic novel with a survivalist theme is **"Lucifer's Hammer"** by David Niven and Jerry Pournel, Fawcett Crest Books, 1977. Within it is a poignant scene of a RAND physicist wrapping his library, book by book, in multiple plastic bags, treated with insecticides, and burying them in his backyard septic tank for safe keeping until a cataclysmic crisis has passed. His books become the basis for a re-emerging civilization's knowledge base.

You should buy how-to-do books. In the resources section of each chapter, I have listed the very best general books I know as sources of self sufficiency and survival information. Many of these may be ordered through UFD's mail order service. You should also haunt used book stores and flea markets and yard sales.

HOME SCHOOLING SUPPLIES AND RE-SOURCES

Christian parents will not be able to use public schooling if they reject the mark. They are going to need materiels if they are going to teach their children at home.

SILVER COINS
One of the most knowledgeable self-sufficiency experts I know is Carl Krupp— publisher and main writer of the "World's Largest Newsletter", **Self-Reliant Living**. He recently wrote an excellent column on the importance of keeping pre-1967 (all real silver) junk coins. In this context, junk means coins with no collectible value beyond face value or the worth of their silver content. Carl graciously allowed me to quote from his column.

SILVER AND GOLD
In times of trouble people stop trusting printed currency with no underlying value, such as our dollar bills. They only want to take "real money" such as silver coins and bars, and gold coins.

Of course, your goal should be that you will not have to buy anything during such times, but there will always be some exceptions you will want to make. Suppose your neighbor decides he wants to sell the 40 acres next to you that includes a nice stream and pond. You might want to add it to your property enough that you would be willing to give up 1 / 3 of your silver and gold reserves. It would all depend.

INVESTMENT DECISIONS
Right now gold is selling for under $400 per once and many of the Gurus say it will hit $700-800 within three years. Silver is selling for under $4 per ounce and they say it will hit $125. This means that gold can go up 2 times while silver may go up 30 times! Naturally we favor silver as the investment to make now.

We agree with the gurus, in part because the price of gold is being controlled by the Soviet - Arab - U.S. businessmen, allowed to only float just so high before they dump their huge reserves onto the market. They are doing this to convert their gold to cash, without depressing the gold market. They have so far not bothered with silver, since it is bulkier to store than gold!

Should the expected inflation of silver and gold occur then silver would turn out to be the perfect solution. Right now a bag of $1,000 pre '67 common silver quarters is selling for $3,050. Should silver climb to just $50 an ounce, which it has already done once in this decade, a bag of silver coins would be worth $35,000!

If times get really bad, such as they were in the Great Depression, then junk silver coins will also prove to be the best investment anyone could make, used one at a time for small purchases, or by the $1,000 face amount bag for large purchases.

OUR PERSONAL PREDICTION
We happen to agree that within five years, silver will be selling for at least $50 an ounce.

If that prediction comes true, just two bags of silver coins, which today cost $6,100, would be worth $70,000! If the Gurus are right, and silver actually hits $125 per ounce, then two bags of coins would be worth $175,000.

We do not believe anything else will inflate as fast as junk silver coins, and highly recommend you buy a bag or two.

Questionable Items

There are two other types of items which survivalists recommend highly for bartering—booze and tobacco. My church warns against the use of such goods. You'll have to follow your own belief system on this. If I were to use these as bartering supplies, I would be going against what I believe to be valid spiritual guidance. I would become the equivalent of a "pusher" to those who see nothing wrong in their use. They would have great potential worth. Only you can decide whether you should stockpile such items.

SKILLED / UNSKILLED SERVICES AND LABOR

Most of you may have at least one skill area

ompetency. Seek to broaden the skills you know and to improve the depth of what you know best. Learn to work with your hands. Understanding the mating habits of Siamese fighting fish may wow oceanographers; however, knowing how to compost may have more value to your survival and to others. The more skill at self sufficiency you gain, the more you'll be able to trade your labor and skills for your own needs.

INVESTMENT STRATEGIES

Most of us are not independently wealthy. We have finite resources and must prioritize the use of our money. What should we focus on first? I cannot claim to be an expert financial consultant; however, I can give you the sum total of advice I have heard from a number of experts. I can also provide a common sense approach which makes sense to me. The priority of expenditures, as I see it, should be as follows:

- Get debt free.
- Purchase food staples and acquire the ability to grow your own.
- Pay off your mortgage.
- Round out the rest of your home storage for personal use.
- Acquire bartering items.
- Pre-pay taxes and assessments.
- Get off the power grid.

These items are not necessarily serial in nature. It's possible to work on several, if not all, of these areas simultaneously. It is prioritized so that one can insure the more important areas are covered as soon as possible.

"What happens if none of this comes to pass?", you might ask. Well, living debt free and self sufficiently is not an unwise lifestyle. I've had accountants look at me in horror when I've mentioned paying off my mortgage. They tend to think only in terms of tax deductions and shelters. They obviously have never gone through a depression. I see this life style as building in your own insurance program and golden parachute. If you can sacrifice for 3-4 years, you might find yourselves in a position where you don't really need too much money to live a fairly comfortable lifestyle. If the worst case happens, you'll be ready.

You'll notice I didn't mention retirement plans or education funds. No man knows the exact date of the second coming; however, I think we can bracket it fairly well. I have friends who live in a rose-tinted world. One man, a highly intelligent Army colonel, recently told me he didn't think the tribulations would come for 200 years. I marvel at attitudes such as this, given the signs of the times. This exemplifies what I call the "ostrich syndrome". People don't like to think about bad things which could happen to them.

I believe the bad times will be on us very soon. Remember, the Bible tells us we will have a total of seven years of bad times, divided into two 42-month periods. The first period will be dedicated toward setting up the structure (New World Order) and the second will be the actual rule of the

Surviving Global Slavery

Anti-Christ. I hesitate to nail down an exact starting date; however, there are numerous indications which say that the New World Order's programmed degradation of our society and economy will probably culminate around 1994. I don't believe this is a hard, firm date; however, I am using it as a personal planning point. If you think it incorrect, develop your own, but make sure you work toward it. If the time is that short, retirement and higher education plans may become moot. Now, let me address how you might successfully attain the goals which will allow you to survive the tribulations.

GETTING OUT OF DEBT AND BECOMING MORTGAGE FREE

Living debt-free is simply a smart way to do business. Pay off any auto loans, credit cards, revolving charge accounts, as quickly as possible and refrain from using credit again. Larry Burkett spends a whole book going over the importance of this concept in his [3] **The Coming Economic Earthquake**.

Paying off a mortgage is a little more difficult but not impossible. The secret is paying additional money out toward the loan's principle. As an illustration, let me use my own situation. We and the bank own a commercial building in downtown Leavenworth where our bookstore and publishing company are located. We just recently bought a modest house with 2.7 acres just outside of the city limits. We owe approximately $35,000 on the building which will be paid for in ten years.

48

Commerce and Economics

We owe approximately $65,000 on the house with a twenty-year loan. I have been putting $190 a month into a government IRA-type savings account. This year gave me a $130 per month cost of living raise. This is the strategy we plan to use to pay off these mortgages early:

1. Cancel my allotment into the government savings plan. Pool that money with my raise to place $300 per month in a savings account in our bank. Apply this $3,600 per year toward the store loan's principle. The payoff period is cut down to three years on the $35,000 loan balance. This really demonstrates how much of mortgage payments are dedicated to interest payments. By reducing the principle even slightly, there is an exponential payoff in shortening that loan payoff period. The key is to do it systematically.

2. Once the commercial building is paid for, the money which we used to pay on its loan plus the $3,600 per year savings will be applied toward the house's loan principle. This will pay off the house in another three and a half years.

3. The overall game plan is to be free and clear of both mortgages in 3 and 6.5 years, instead of in 10 and 20 years respectfully.

These figures will vary as to interest rates, loan payoff periods, and the amounts placed against principles. If you have a home computer, there are a number of cheap or free public domain financial planning programs which will allow you to analyze how best to do this for yourselves. If you don't

49

feel comfortable doing this, try to find a friend who can.

AFORDABILITY STRATEGIES

The way to finance getting out of debt and other purchases, beyond the immediate means of your salary, could include:

1. Selling off unneeded belongings (we tend to collect far too many material things over time.) If you haven't used an item in the past 2-5 years, maybe you don't really need it.

2. Giving food storage gifts at Christmas and birthdays. Can you think of any more loving gift than future survival.

3. Sacrifice dining out as a family. We tend to eat fairly cheaply, yet the four of us rarely get by for less than $25-30 at the local family restaurants. That amount will buy over 200 pounds of wheat, two-thirds of an adult's yearly grain requirement. The same holds true for recreational spending such as movies, videos, ball games, plays, family vacations or dances. I'm not suggesting you have no fun, just find ways to do it for free or cheaply. How much time do we have, brothers and sisters? Are you willing to gamble that it's later than sooner?

4. If you currently support a habit which is less than life enhancing, such as tobacco, alcohol, or excessive soft drinks, drop the habit cold-turkey and start spending the money saved on getting

Commerce and Economics

ready for the coming bad times.

5. Get a part-time job or start a business on the side.

6. Prioritize your miscellaneous spending. I'm guilty of impulse buying of neat little things for the house. I'm having to watch that now.

7. Make do with what you've got. Don't buy a new car or truck every three years. Its cheaper to keep it fixed up. A new van today costs as much ($25,500) as my first house in Falls Church, Virginia, back in 1973.

PREPAYING TAXES AND ASSESSMENTS

"Alright, Bob, what are you smoking? Are you saying to pay my taxes in advance?" Yes, certain ones. If you have your house and land paid for and you think your self-sufficiency supplies are in pretty good shape, you might try to take away the one weapon the government could still hold to your head. Of course I'm speaking primarily about property taxes. If you can pay these in advance, say for the next ten years, you can probably safely reject the mark and not have to worry about the government confiscating your home for non-payment of taxes.

I would imagine your community will not be ready for such an action (it might mess up their bureaucratic procedures); therefore, I recommend you seek advice from your attorney or a good tax accountant on how best to go about this. They'll

51

probably try to talk you out of it, suggesting you put your money in savings or escrow and pay the taxes as they come due. They may not understand that you're not trying to make more money, but are trying to save your family's future. Stick to your guns! An escrow account might work, it all depends on how you will be perceived if you reject the mark. You may become a non-person, not allowed to conduct commerce through others, such as banks.

If you can talk your community into going along with a pre- payment, make sure you get an agreement in writing that you will not be asked for additional taxes in that period. Otherwise, this may be all for nought.

GETTING OFF THE POWER GRID

If you can't pay your utility bills, you won't be able to use commercially provided electricity or gas. Start planning now for alternative energy sources to live on. This will be covered in detail in chapter 10.

A WORD OF WARNING

Dear brothers and sisters in Christ, time works against us. Please don't delay getting your house in order. By the time many of you get out of debt and mortgage free, you should have a pretty clear idea of the New World Order's pace. If they are well on the way to officially employing a global government, you have the option of continuing preparations or not. It's better to be safe than sorry.

Commerce and Economics

RESOURCES

1. **Called to Serve** by James "Bo" Gritz, Lazarus Publishing Co., 1991, $25.00.

2. **Journal for Self-Reliant Living**, P.O. Box 910, Merlin, OR 97532, $72 for one year and $132 for two years.

3. **The Coming Economic Earthquake** by Larry Burkett, Moody Press, 1991, $14.95.

4. **MINMAC Custom Ammunition**, 8201 Highway 138, Oakland, OR 97462, (503) 459-5188.

5. **Precision Hardcast Bullets**, (reloading supplier), 4885 Industrial Dr., Springfield, IL 62703, (800) 325-4492.

6. **AAA-ARMS & AMMO**, 4877 S. 135th St, Omaha, NE 68137, (402) 896-8254.

Surviving Global Slavery

CHAPTER 3
FAMILIES

The New World Order and Satan would destroy the nuclear family. Well-knit family units make individuals difficult to control. Take children away from their families early on and it's much easier to program their attitudes and ethics for the ulterior motive of those in power. By disrupting the family, Satan creates chaos.

If there is a political/philosophical operating system in the New World Order, it is Liberalism. Although many of those who pull the strings behind the scenes are apolitical (ie. self-oriented), their significant social engineering tool is liberal actions. They use people professing these beliefs to rip apart the fabric of society. When at long last a conservative backlash takes place, they can cause amazing governmental changes toward tighter controls to deal with the problems created by the liberals. They become the real winners in the end because tighter controls by a government structure owned by these people effectively means they have more power and dominion over the world.

To gain an appreciation of how this can affect the family, we need to understand how people of these two persuasions think and feel. If you're a liberal, you will tend to see the traditional family unit as a restrictive threat. Charles C. Heath states in his book, [1] **The Blessings of Liberty**, "Because they see human depravity originating outside the individual, liberals see less need for the restraining influence of religion or traditional family structures. In fact, they often see these institutions as the source of the problem. Feminists, for example, see the traditional family as a repressive institution, limiting the freedom of women (and men) by imposing on them stereotypical roles that stifle their development. Once these oppressive structures and the roles they foster are destroyed, individuals (especially women) will be free to develop in whatever way expresses their individuality. Hence, feminists welcome the disintegration of the family and eagerly embrace alternative arrangements, from state-run child care to allowing homosexuals to marry and adopt children."

"Conservatives, by contrast, see the family as an institution that evolved in response to human nature, not something that stifles or deforms that nature. Liberals have it backwards. The family is not the result of a conspiracy by men to oppress women; it reflects fundamental human needs and aspirations felt by men and women, the need for each other and a suitable environment in which to raise children. Reproducing itself and nurturing the next generation is, after all, the fundamental human task, and the family has evolved in response to this fundamental need."

Families are Heavenly Father's plan. He developed the family model by the way he deals through Jesus Christ with us, his children. Our spiritual family is based on love and nurturing, growth and development within a stable framework which has set standards and boundaries of right and wrong. These exist, not to stifle us, but to allow his spiritual children to grow, develop, and mature with a ready reference of guidelines.

Satan hates this loving relationship with our Heavenly Father and Jesus. After all, he was thrown out of that relationship long ago for his rebellion. Is it any wonder he is doing his utmost to destroy loving and caring relations amongst those of us on this earthly plane? The New World Order embodies the fuzziest of Liberal (and Satanic) thinking in its value systems. Those behind the power structure realize the importance of the concept, divide and conquer. If they can get children to "do their own thing", they can create the ultimate consumer. This is just good business to them. They are apolitical and amoral. They only care about manipulating the rest of mankind for their own selfish purposes.

STRATEGIES

First and foremost, your survival through the coming bad times may well depend on the strength and resources of your immediate and extended family. I expect, for example, that my son and my oldest daughter may want to bring their spouses to live with or near us during the final days so that we may pool our resources and our strength and talents. My father-in-law feels the same way. There is strength and unity within families which pull together.

How can you create that kind of unity in family groups these days when it seems the whole world is trying to tear them asunder? Here are some common sense steps your family can take which will help cement stronger, God-based relationships.

Daily Scripture Reading and Prayer

Every night, just before bedtime, our family members gather around and take turns reading a chapter of the scriptures together out loud. We parents will often interrupt the reading to ask questions or make comments to insure our younger ones are really understanding what is going on. We then kneel down in prayer and go around the family circle with individual prayers. These are not rote memorized cute prayers like, "Now I lay me down to sleep." Instead, we use an open format. First, the individual praying thanks his or her Heavenly Father for the blessings and assistance received that day. Next, we petition for additional help or blessings needed to make it through the next day or so. Finally, we acknowledge our request through Jesus Christ, and close with an Amen.

It is absolutely amazing how true feelings and concerns sometimes surface. It is especially wonderful to hear one of the children express love and a need for a blessing on another one, forgetting

Families

himself in the process. Oft-times, brothers and sisters come to a realization that others in the family really care for them. They don't have to face their problems alone.

This is definitely bonding time for us. Normally this activity lasts about fifteen minutes. It is essential scripture reading and prayer become a routine. They should never be skipped, even if it's very late. When that happens, we may only read a verse each and say our prayers, but we don't miss it. If someone is sick in the family, we gather around that person's bed. If someone forgot and started taking a bath, we may gather in the bathroom with the shower curtains closed, but there is no escaping this event. It is remarkable what a stabilizing factor this has become in our spiritual life. It's also great how well we all come to better understand the scriptures.

FAMILY COUNCILS

Once a week, we gather together to have a very short spiritual lesson, sing a hymn or two, and discuss family chores, problems, and so on. Self-sufficiency requires work. This is the time to address what needs to be accomplished during the coming week; who should do what tasks with whom; why it needs to be done, and what are the hoped for results. It is in this manner everyone becomes personally involved. Then we try to do a fun activity together (preferably with refreshments).

How many families do you know who really

take the time to have quality family experiences together. This won't solve all your problems; however, it will go a long way toward preventing some. Besides, it's just a good leadership practice. Keep the troops informed and personally involved. We also allow the children's opinions to be heard and involve them in the decision-making process. It is how family strength and pride are built.

We try to set aside Sunday or Monday nights for this. Everyone understands they must work their busy schedules around this time.

EAT MEALS TOGETHER

I know mothers who serve as many as three or four dinners in one night as the kids come and go to various activities. This is Satan's way. Dinner time should be a moment for all to sit down together to eat, share their day's experiences, and to communicate one with another. Again, this gets difficult to do with all the demands on everyones' time. You need to prioritize family first whenever possible.

Oh yes, if you're just starting these programs, you're going to hear a lot of whining and complaining. Stick to your guns, mom and dad! Once they become a routine, once the kids see you're really serious about doing them, they'll be disappointed if you don't spend these times together.

Families

TURN OFF THE TV

Granted, many will go into immediate withdrawal pains. In fact, television has become a drug— a true opiate of the masses. The average American family spends more time in front of the boob-tube than they spend in school or at work. If you think about it, though, how much is really worth watching anymore?

This doesn't mean never to watch TV again. Be selective in what you watch and how many hours are spent doing it. I'll never forget my son's reaction to a rather drastic remedy I was forced to take during his early high school years.

I had instructed the kids to leave the television off when they got home from school so they could get their homework done right away. My wife worked at our bookstore and I came home from my government job each afternoon. The kids usually beat me home by half an hour or so.

They could hear my car coming up the driveway, so they would watch TV and listen for me. By the time I came through the door, the TV was off and they were in their rooms. Having been a kid once myself, I suspected something like this had been going on when it seemed they still had a lot of home work to do. All I had to do was feel the TV. If it was warm to the touch, I knew they had been watching it. (Dads can be sneaky too.)

I called my son in to the family room with his sisters. I confronted him with what had been

61

going on and pulled out a pair of wire cutters. You should have seen his face when I cut the power cord in two. He looked as if I'd just poured a kilo of cocaine down the drain. The cord stayed cut for a month until I wanted to watch the olympic games. His sisters also let him know they didn't appreciate the consequences of his behavior.

People often ask me, how do I manage to do so many activities. I tell them it's easy. I just don't watch much TV. Its fantastic what one can crowd into life without spending all of it in front of the idiot box. Because of this approach, my kids love to read for pleasure. They get personally involved with the family, and TV becomes something the family watches together occasionally. Parents, don't let it become your electronic baby sitter. If you don't monitor what's being seen, you've opened up Hell's doors. The television is one of Satan's primary tools for reprogramming people of all ages.

When people ask me what's wrong with the youth today, I answer, "We're dealing with a lost generation— one which has been raised by the media and their peers. We have too many latchkey children who have been taught ethics from a video screen and their buddies."

Is it any wonder we have a youth gang problem? The most powerful recruiting tool the gangs have is their offering of themselves as a surrogate family. Why should our children feel a void in this area? If you begin the programs outlined above, I promise you they will make a

Families

positive difference in your family. Fill that void!

RESOURCES

1. **The Blessings of Liberty** by Charles C. Heath, Huntington House Publishers, 1991, $8.95.

Surviving Global Slavery

CHAPTER 4
EMERGENCY
PREPAREDNESS

For many who read survivalist literature, this topic usually implies being ready for natural disasters or nuclear attacks. That hasn't changed; however, I'd like to add another aspect— escape from police state authorities. If you reject the mark, you might find them knocking at your door some night. If you get a forewarning, will you be ready to grab and go?

Whatever the reason, it is important to be able to grab a pack and head out the door with the wherewithal to survive away from home for at least three days and nights. In case of a disaster, it generally takes most communities at least 2-3 days to ramp up their emergency infrastructure. In case of an escape from authorities, it may take that long to get to safety. Keeping enough food, water, tenting, and clothing on hand, is a good insurance policy.

As a military family, we've had to do this all over the world. In case the balloon went up, my family was always ready to grab their emergency

65

kits and head for the evacuation point. In Seoul, Korea, we knew that the family might have to walk south the entire length of the Korean peninsula to Pusan in the event of a North Korean attack. We kept our emergency packs on hand and actually wore them on weekend hikes to become accustomed to their weight.

What you pack in your seventy-two hour kit may vary as to your family's needs. The following are lists of recommended basic items. I would also suggest you pack an additional one week's worth of food and clothing supplies for everyone in one duffle bag. This gives you an option. If you have time and can transport the extra bag, you might want to bring it along just in case.

Basic 72-hour kit requirements:

- Container for your kit
- Water (and water purification supplies)
- Food
- Shelter
- Bedding
- Clothing
- Fire starters
- First Aid kit
- Misc comfort items
- Family Information Record

I should stress these are the bare minimum basics. You can get as fancy as you want, assuming you can carry it all. Don't presume you'll have a vehicle. You might have to walk, so make every ounce count.

Emergency Preparedness

Kit Containers

Some people like to store their kits in 5-gallon plastic buckets (the kind used by painters, bakeries, etc). Since the buckets have sealable lids, they are convenient for keeping their contents safe from harm. They also store conveniently and are stackable. They are, however, better suited for vehicle transportation. Plastic buckets with metal bails are awkward and tiring to carry.

We use back packs. They don't have to be super expensive. They could be cheap discount store specials or even homemade. With the military down-sizing so much, you'll probably be able to pick up some excellent army surplus bargains. We also use army duffle bags. The more modern ones have pack straps sewn onto them already and can carry an amazing amount of weight and volume. Both are easy to fix up so they are water resistant. Line their interiors with plastic trash bags and tie shut tightly once filled. Then, shut the pack flaps over them.

Water

We keep a pistol belt (military web belt), with two military canteens already attached for each person in the family. We plan to fill the canteens from faucets or from our family's emergency water storage supplies before leaving. These, and other military items, are easily found at army surplus stores and gun and knife shows. We also pack several 1-gallon collapsible water jugs without water and water purification tablets so we can stock up on water once we get to our escape meeting place.

Food

The perfect food for a emergency preparedness 72-hour kit is the military's Meal, Ready to Eat ration, or MRE. They can be found at any number of surplus and emergency preparedness outfitters (see this chapter's resource section for a sampling of addresses.) They have a 7-10 year shelf life and come in cases of 12. Depending on who's selling them, they should cost $45-$60 per case. We got lucky with a source and bought a case for $30. A meal comes in a water proof plastic pouch with additional items such as toilet paper. They are light weight and convenient to pack.

If you don't want to go the MRE route, it's ok to pack regular food. Make out a menu for three days and pack accordingly. Rotate your emergency food stocks every six months. Microwavable spaghetti meals, ramen soup, peanut butter, crackers, one-a-day multiple vitamins, etc., are all excellent items. Remember, these packs are for emergencies, so don't break into them to use the food when you've run short in day to day situations. You could easily forget to replace them and will be sorry (and hungry) when an emergency arises.

Don't forget mess kits or plasticware. You may need to include a few pots and pans as well.

Emergency Preparedness

Although more expensive, packing MREs makes much of this superfluous.

Shelter

Whether you pack elaborate back-packer tents, a tarpolan and rope, or small individual tents called "Tube Tents", you'll need to bring something which keeps rain, snow, and wind off your sleeping family.

Bedding

Like food, it's better to err on the side of too much rather than too little. We pack moderate winter climate military sleeping bags for our region's climate. If you're in a tropical area, you may need much less. Wherever you live, insect netting and lotion should also be included. We also pack light-weight sleeping pads (I've never had much luck with air mattresses).

Clothing

Durable clothing such as jeans, military fatigues, work pants and shirts, and so on are the safest bet. A good rain poncho or rain suit for each person is important if your climate has rain. Work gloves, heavy socks, and a stocking hat are also helpful items. If you have children, remember to keep abreast of their growing spurts. Large is better than small. Heavy hiking boots and rubber boots are best for the feet. Make sure you have several changes of everything, to include underwear.

Surviving Global Slavery

Fire Starters

Kitchen matches tied in a bundle and dipped into melted paraffin store dry and will light under just about any conditions. A small can of lighter fluid is helpful. We pour melted paraffin wax into <u>paper</u> egg carton containers filled with lint from the clothes dryer or other such tinder. When the wax has hardened, we cut the egg crate sections apart. Each one makes a fantastic fire starter.

First Aid Kit

There are any number of good kits available. Most are designed to carry around in your car. You may want more items than that. Again, gun and knife shows usually have vendors who sell medical utensils at reasonable prices. You should probably include a snake-bite kit. Rubber surgical gloves are definitely a must these days with the AIDS threat. It wouldn't be wise to get a stranger's blood on you. Various emergency supply houses sell from simple to very complete medical kits. (See the resources section.)

Remember to include supplies of any required prescription drugs and extra pairs of eye glasses. A supply of over the counter drugs should also be considered, such as anti-histamines, aspirins/tylonol, etc.

Misc Comfort Items

If there are females of menstruating age in

Emergency Preparedness

your group, remember hygiene supplies. A bonus is the fact that feminine napkins also make great compress bandages. Bug spray, sun block, compass, and area maps are typical of items which can make the difference between surviving or not.

One of the best all around item which will accomplish several different functions is the heavy duty plastic trash bag. For example, cut three holes in a big one and you have a small rain coat. It will keep clothes dry, haul garbage, and even act as a ground cloth. Make sure each person has a couple rolls of toilet paper. Carry a small entrenching tool (fold-up camp shovel) on your belt so you can dig an individual latrine (called a cat hole) as needed.

Family Information Record

Carry information about everybody in your group. Typical helpful data are: Blood type and Rh factor, allergies, wills, pictures of each person (in case someone becomes lost or taken, searchers will know who they're looking for and what they look like). Information about relatives or God parents might be important if all the adults die for some reason. Shot records and identification papers might also be helpful.

RESOURCES

1. **Emergency Survival Packs** by Blair D. Jaynes, Horizon Publishers, $4.95.

2. **Emergency Preparedness Handbook** by Gary Barnes, 1992, $14.95.

3. **NITRO-PACK Catalog**. This is the best mailorder source of preparedness items in terms of quality and availability. We recommend them highly! A good source for MREs! $3.00, see our order blank (good toward your first purchase)

CHAPTER 5
HOME STORAGE

"But if any provide not for his own, and specially for those of his own house, he hath denied the faith, and is worse than an Infidel." 1 Timothy 5:8

One of the best investments one can make, regardless of whether the end-times are here or not, is on a good home storage program. Our elderly brothers and sisters understand this idea. Many of them lived through the harsh years of the great depression. They know what it is like to go hungry. At the time of this writing, I am forty-six, almost forty-seven years old. Generally, my generation had it pretty good. My peers and those younger than us don't know what it's like to go through really hard times.

I was working on a church service project recently, helping out the local Big Brothers/Big Sisters program by painting playground equipment. Their director, a sweet lady, lived with her Baptist missionary grandparents when she was young. She and I compared notes on our respective childhoods. I had grown up on a self-sufficient

Surviving Global Slavery

Quaker farm near Kokomo, Indiana until I was seven. She had grown up in British Honduras, forced into self-sufficiency by the poverty of their mission. We both commented on how unusual we were to have had to depend on growing our own food and canning it for later use. I recalled what it was like to watch my grandfather transition from work horses to tractors on his 360 acre farm. Food storage was a way of life to us. I may have hated working in the "truck patch" as a young boy, but I sure liked the food it produced.

How many of us are truly dependant on what we grow or raise to eat today? Yet, how dependable is the food system we have learned to trust? The fragility of our food chain was drastically brought home to my parents back in the seventies. A great blizzard had hit Indiana. All the highways and streets were closed. My dad noticed they were out of milk but couldn't back his car out of the driveway because the snow was drifted too deeply. He got out of his car and began to wade his way the two short blocks to the grocery store. When he got there, he discovered there was no milk in the cooler. He ended up buying the last box of powdered milk. The store's shelves had been almost cleared in just a few hours by panicked shoppers.

Under normal conditions, stores usually carry no more than three to ten days supply of stock for the population segment they support. During times of emergency, panic buyers can strip the shelves in a few moments.

Home Storage

The food chain is vulnerable at several points. Our small farmers are going down the economic tubes all over the country. Who will replace them? Weather has been going crazy. Drought could easily have a major impact on the food chain. The Bible graphically talks about terrible famines in the last days. Revelations 16:21 says, *"And there fell upon men a great hail out of heaven, every stone about the weight of a talent: and men blasphemed God because of the plague thereof was exceeding great."* Perhaps that hail will destroy most of our crops.

Matthew 24:7-8 states, *"For nation shall rise against nation, and kingdom against kingdom: and there shall be famines, and pestilences, and earthquakes, in divers places. All these are the beginning of sorrows."*

In addition to these natural catastrophes adversely impacting the food chain, we will see possible oil and gas shortages because of wars and rumors of wars. Fuel cutbacks mean transportation cutbacks. It was transportation cutbacks due to the weather which brought about the denuding of the grocery shelves near my father's home.

What to Store

"OK, Bob, I'm convinced. I see where home storage might be important, but what do I need to store and how do I do it?" To answer this we will examine:
- Food Storage
- Gardening

Surviving Global Slavery

- Water Storage and Purification
- Heating, Cooking, and Lighting
- Clothing

Food Storage

First off, lets not make this any more diffi-cult than it need be. Going out and buying a couple of freezer chests full of frozen meats and vege-tables is not the answer. Freezers defrost when the electricity shuts off. Then you'll have to race against time to make one heck of a lot of jerky. Nor do you want to buy mostly canned goods, which do not remain nutritious over time and tend to go bad (especially if they are acidic). Freeze dried food is expensive, but definitely a viable option in terms of shelf and nutritional life. There is a less expen-sive, more practical approach, however.

The key to sensible food storage is the same now as it was in past centuries. Your program should be built around dry staples. By this we mean such things as grains, legumes (beans), sugar/honey, salt, baking supplies, dried dairy products, fats and oils. These items are relatively cheap, easy to store for long periods, and are relatively compact. A year's supply of staples such as these which would guarantee an adult female 2,300 calories per day can be had for a little over $300. Of course, this is not all one should eat. You should supplement them with fresh and canned garden produce and any number of meat possibili-ties.

Do you have to have meat? No, but you do

need to know what you're doing, if you're going to take the totally vegetarian route. Vegetable proteins are incomplete. It is important to know that there are two kinds of vegetable proteins. These must be eaten during the same meal to allow them to combine in your body to form a complete protein with all the amino acids, etc. it takes to insure they do their nutritional job. Fortunately, this is not difficult to do. Generally, grains and legumes combine into complete vegetable proteins. Knowing this will allow you to plan your family's meals appropriately.

Lets take a look at what an adult female's yearly supply of staples consists of. You can add to or cut back these amounts proportionately to figure adult male, teenagers, and small childrens' requirements; however, we recommend that you use the adult female planning figure for everyone as a fudge factor. In this business it's better to be safe than sorry. You should store:

• **300 lbs. of Grains**. This includes wheat, rice, corn, popcorn, oat meal, barley, and pasta. Since our family has spent a fair amount of time in the orient, we eat a lot of rice and keep on hand around 700-800 lbs. at all times. You might prefer more corn dishes, while others may really like pasta or wheat. The key is to store proportionally to your family's eating habits. Times of hardship and stress are not when you should be introducing new food to the kids. Make these a part of your day to day living now. Besides, this is a healthy way to eat.

Surviving Global Slavery

Our family also stores about 1200 pounds of wheat, 300 pounds of corn, 200 lbs of rolled oats, and 100 lbs of barley. We soon plan to add soybeans, since we've found a couple of good recipes for making bean curds or tofu. It's important to note we store enough grain for two years (soon to be expanded to four years) for the four of us living at home. We also store and eat this variety of grain to relieve food boredom.

We've listed a source (NITRO-PAK) of grains already treated and packed by specialty companies in the resource section. However, if you live anywhere near a farm community, you can buy much of this from a granary or a feed store. As far as wheat is concerned, we buy re-cleaned hard winter wheat seed. It must be the hard variety to insure ease of milling or grinding. It also has the best protein content.

• **150 lbs. of Legumes (Beans)**. This includes all kinds of beans, peanuts, and peanut butter. Again, we store a large variety of these. We especially like to eat corn bread made from freshly ground corn meal along with our bean dishes, thus providing a complete protein.

• **100 lbs. of Dairy Products**. This includes powdered milk & cheese, and canned evaporated milk. Milk products are the most volatile of all the food storage items. How they're stored makes a big difference as to their shelf life.

• **100 lbs. of Flour**.

Home Storage

- **100 lbs. of Sugar or Honey.**

- **2 gal. Cooking Oil or Shortening**

- **5 lbs. Salt** (we recommend more if you plan to use salt for meat and hide preservation). Soy sauce is an excellent salt source and is a good flavoring for jerky.

- **1 lbs. Baking Powder**

- **365 One-A-Day Multiple Vitamins** (To insure you get all your nutrients. These should be rotated yearly, month by month, to insure maximum potency).

- **Garden Seeds.** We recommend you store original seed stock rather than the hybrid seeds sold in most stores. Hybrids do not breed true. You may get a wonderful garden this year, but if you use the seeds from this year's crop, next year's garden won't look anything like what came up this year. See the resource section for the addresses of two recognized seed banks which carry original seed stocks.

- **Home Canning**. Buy enough canning jars, rings, and lids to can your garden's excess produce. Remember you will need far more lids than rings because they cannot be reused while the rings can be. See the resources section for canning how-to books.

In addition, you should consider storing these other stocks:

Surviving Global Slavery

• **Canned Food**. It's ok to store canned goods; however, we recommend keeping only about a 6-month stock on hand. Beware of buying canned food at sale prices. Oft times stores place canned goods which are about to go out of date on sale. Let the buyer beware, read the labels or ask the stock clerks. See Appendix A for plans to build a vertical canned goods storage system which rotates your stock automatically.

You might try to locate a food-buying co-operative in your area, or start one yourself. For guidance and a source of products write, **The Blooming Prairie Warehouse, 2340 Heinz Road, Iowa City, IA 52240.**

• **Dehydrated/Freeze Dried/Nitrogen-Packed Food**. These have excellent shelf lives, are compact, and are, therefore, easy to store. They are also very expensive. See the resource section for the best sources of these foods.

• **Toilet Paper and Other Sanitary Supplies**. Determine how much toilet paper your family goes through in a day and a week. Stock up whenever there is a sale. Check out the generic brands. Sometimes, they are cheaper everyday than the name brands on sale. If there are ladies in the house of menstrual age, stock up on those supplies, or be prepared to use and reuse rags in the same manner as women did in the old days.

• **Meat**. The best ways to preserve meat is to smoke or dry it. See the resource section for the

Home Storage

best books which tell how to do this.

> • **Dried Fruit and Vegetables**. It is fairly easy to dehydrate fruits and vegetables at home. See the resource section for the best sources on how to do this.

Food Storage

There are several important considerations when storing large amounts of food. These include:

1. **The Quality of Products**. Obtain the best quality of food possible and store it away from other products which may affect the flavor.

2. **Proper Containers**. Use heavy plastic or metal storage containers with sealable lids. Ofttimes weevils (little worms and bugs) can be a problem. Their eggs are in the products already. (If you don't believe me, set aside a sealed box of crackers or a sack of flour for a year. When you open them, you will find little worms crawling around in the food. The same goes for pasta). Some people may be pretty squeamish about that, although the worms may add a little protein to your diet. It is possible to provide an atmosphere which will insure their death immediately upon hatching, and we will discuss this in paragraph 7 below. We use 4 and 5-gal plastic buckets for dry packing and roll-around plastic garbage cans for items such as corn.

3. **Storage facilities**. The best places to store

Surviving Global Slavery

long-term food supplies are those which remain cool (40-60 degrees), dark, and easy to get to.

4. Rotation. I wasted a lot of money the first time I stockpiled canned goods from the grocery. I got lazy and didn't rotate my stock. Also, my store room wasn't cooled. Within six months, I had whole cases of bulging cans of food which had to be thrown away.

5. Ventilation. Use storage areas which are well ventilated, dark, clean, and dry, as well as cool. Basements and root cellars are great. See the resource section for a book on how to construct a root cellar.

6. Placement. Don't place food storage containers on or against dirt/cement floors or walls. Put your containers on wooden pallets to provide good air circulation and to keep them dry.

7. Dry Packing. Items such as grains, beans, non-fat dry milk, and dried vegetables can be given extra protection during storage. This is done to combat the great enemies of food storage— spoilage due to oxidation and bugs. The idea is to eliminate all or most of the oxygen so the food won't spoil and the bugs suffocate when they hatch.

There are two ways to do this, create a vacuum or replace the air in the container with an inert gas. The first can't be done easily at home, although it is done commercially at an additional cost. The second method can be done at home in

Home Storage

two ways.

The first way involves the use of dry ice, which is frozen carbon dioxide. Drop a 1/4 pound piece of dry ice into the bottom of an airtight plastic bucket. Pour the grain in on top of the ice. Place the lid on the bucket but do not seal it for 5-6 hours, then make it airtight. The only drawback is that dry ice may insert a little dampness into the grain.

The second way is to contact a welding supply company. Purchase a regulator and a hose. Lease a tank filled with either nitrogen or carbon dioxide (nitrogen is preferable). Attach the regulator and hose to the bottle of gas. Place the nozzle of the hose in the bottom of the bucket. Fill the bucket with grain. Turn on the gas at the regulator. Hold an open flame about one inch above the grain. When the flame snuffs out, the gas has filled the bucket. Withdraw the hose with the gas still on. Seal the lid immediately.

Grinders

You'll need to get a grinder for your grain (we have two, just in case). Both metal and stone grinders are available. We prefer stone. An ideal grinder should have the ability to vary the courseness of the grinding. Electric grinders should also have the ability to be operated by hand when there is no electricity. Or, buy one of each kind. Grind just enough grain at a time for a week's usage to obtain the best nutrition and taste.

Surviving Global Slavery

Gardening

It is not the intent of this book to teach you how to garden. We have listed the best books we know on how to garden in the resource section. We do want to take the time to discuss some important philosophical aspects of gardening.

If you have a yard, you've got land which can be gardened. Even if you don't have a yard, it is possible to grow small gardens on roof tops. If you don't own your own land or don't have enough room to garden, try to form a share-cropping relationship with someone who does. Rent land out of town. However you do it, **start gardening!**

Experts say it takes about three years to learn how to garden organically. We stress organic gardening because chemical fertilizers may not be available during the tribulations. Composting, mixing compost into the soil, conditioning clayey soil, etc., learning how to deal with pests and weeds, and learning when to harvest all take time. Don't wait until the tribulations, **start now!**

Start acquiring your gardening equipment immediately. It can be costly. If you can't afford all your own equipment, form a gardening group which either buys or shares their equipment in common. We recommend a minimum of a garden tractor with cart, a rear-tined tiller, a watering system, and a chipper/shredder, plus the usual hand tools such as hoes, rakes, shovels, and trowels. Hand carts, wheel barrows, etc. are also useful.

84

Home Storage

Investigate different gardening methods. For example, this year we are comparing an intensive method with raised beds, called square-foot gardening, with a much larger tiller-cultivated garden with raised rows.

Learn by doing. Consult local experts. Your county farm agent can provide invaluable information about gardening in your area. His services and literature are usually free.

Live Stock

If you or someone in your group has sufficient land, you may want to raise small numbers of livestock for meat sources. We're not talking about expensive feeder-lot operations— rather, a small scale operation which takes advantage of natural feed sources wherever possible. We recommend the following animals as those giving the best bang for the buck:

• **Chickens**. These produce eggs and meat and are cheap to feed. They are able to scrounge food for themselves and require only a little bit of supplemental feeding.

• **Sheep**. They eat grass, produce wool, and provide meat. They are easy to work with and are relatively self-sufficient.

• **Goats**. If you must have milk, this is a much cheaper source than cows. The down side is they are difficult to take care of. They get into everything and can be very destructive.

• **Bees**. These take a minimum of care and produce honey, a valuable commodity. They also are valuable for pollination of crops, especially if you have an orchard. For a little more than $100, you can get started in bee keeping through Sears and Robuck. Experts tell us the "Midnight" strain of bees is very productive. Sears will ship the equipment and even the bees.

If you have the land, (5 acres or more) you can easily become self-sufficient in the food department. Using even a 1/4 acre city lot, you can grow enough produce to supplement your staples storage. I think the real key for those who are not fortunate enough to own their own land, is a gardening co-op or a share-cropper arrangement. There is strength and unity in numbers. Your Church might want to buy some farm land for its members' use as a communal food growing project. Even in inner cities, vacant lots have been reclaimed for food growing. Don't let yourselves be limited by conventions! Seek innovative ways to use all available resources.

I'll never forget my first experience in Germany with gardening. Our troop plane had just touched down at Rhein Main Air Force Base in Frankfurt. On our way into town, our bus passed large fields which had been broken up into small garden plots. Each was fenced and had a small cottage/tool storage building.

Europeans know how to get every bit of use

out of their land because they are so crowded. Koreans, Chinese, and Japanese are the same. Wherever land is at a premium because of dense populations, all available land is put to use for food growing. In Korea, I've seen even the sides of ditches put to use. The point is, we Americans have had it easy. Now we need to look to the rest of the world for lessons on making do with what we've got. What we may feel are bare-bones survival conditions in America, is business as usual in third-world countries.

Water Storage and Purification

A source of dependable water is absolutely essential. It is too difficult to store 1-4 years supply of water; however, you should store two weeks worth in case of emergencies. A family of four should store at least 56 gallons (one gallon per day per person) of pure water. It is easier to store water purification supplies. Lets talk about water storage first, then we'll address water purification.

A water tank would be nice for water storage; however, most people don't have the room. We use old one-gallon apple cider glass jugs and one-liter plastic pop bottles. We used to use plastic milk jugs, but discovered the hard way that they were bio-degradable, springing spontaneous leaks after a while. Thirty-five and 55-gallon plastic drums can be obtained from NITRO-PAK which is listed in the resource section.

Bleach is an excellent water purifier. Use 8

87

drops of liquid bleach in which hypochlorite is the only active ingredient per gallon of water. One teaspoon will treat 5-gallons. Since bleach loses strength over time, rotate your bleach stock. If bleach is one-year-old, double the amount used. If two-years old, do not use. If the water is cloudy, double the amount of bleach. After adding the bleach, stir or shake thoroughly and let stand for 30-45 minutes.

There are a number of other ways to purify water, such as iodine treatment, filtering, boiling, etc.. The best source of information on this is in the **Emergency Preparedness Handbook** listed in the resources section.

Heating, Cooking, and Lighting

Fuel for heating is region dependent. Obvious alternatives are wood, charcoal, coal, propane, and kerosene. If wood is plentiful in your area and you have the means to buy or cut your own, this might be a good way to go. A planning figure for home heating in the Midwest is 5-6 chords of wood. If you cook year round, then more will be required. The harder the wood, the better. A chord is a stack of wood eight feet long, four feet high, and four feet wide. A pickup truck load is generally not a full chord.

Charcoal can be dangerous. Never, ever burn it indoors. **It creates carbon monoxide gas as a by-product which will kill you!**

Coal burns hot and requires special stoves.

Home Storage

Make sure your wood-burner is rated for coal as well as wood before burning it in there.

Kerosene is safe to store and fairly available. We have two kerosene portable burners. Each is capable of heating 800 square feet and will allow the placing of a pan on its top for cooking. One 55-gallon plastic drum will provide fuel enough to last an entire winter if used sparingly. Purchase only K-1 rated kerosene and not diesel fuel (which has dangerous additives).

Propane is also an excellent fuel, but is somewhat expensive and requires large storage tanks.

Cooking can be done with all the heating fuels plus sterno and white gas (Coleman fuel). If you're going to cook with wood or coal, you might want to invest in a wood-burning stove. I remember my grandmother putting out some awesome meals for all the farm workers on just such a stove. There is an art to controlling their temperature, so buy soon and learn how to use one before the bad times come. The resource section lists an Amish supply company in Ohio which sells and ships them.

Another good investment you can make is in a set of cast iron dutch ovens and other cast iron cooking wares. See the resource section for a catalog.

Light can be provided by kerosene lanterns, fireplaces, stoves with windows on them, and by candles.

Clothing

Haunt the yard and garage sales for sturdy work clothes. If you have children, remember you're buying for their future use. Try to anticipate how big and fast they grow. Concentrate on denim jeans and military fatigues, and any other similarly well-made clothing.

Learn to sew if you don't know how. This means you too guys! I used to do needle point when I was only six or seven. It didn't make a sissy out of me, but it did teach me a valuable survival skill. I do buttons better than any of my girls.

RESOURCES

1. **Emergency Preparedness Handbook** by Gary Barnes, 1992, $14.95. This is by far the best work on the subject of preparedness.

2. **Reader's Digest Back to Basics** edited by Norman Mack, Readers Digest, 1981, $26.00. This is the best single source of information on the skills needed for homesteading I know. It's considerably better than the Foxfire series and it's all in one book.

3. **Emergency Survival Packs** by Blair D. Jaynes, Horizon Publishing, 1982, $4.95. This useful pamphlet tells how to prepare portable family emergency evacuation kits which could

sustain family members for 72 hours or a 14-day period if they suddenly had to leave their home. It provides a basic family checklist plus lists for various aged children.

4. **Prepare Today— Survive Tomorrow** by Joe Harold, Horizon Publishing, 1984, $11.95. Written in a conservative tone by a seasoned survivalist, this guide provides essential information on raising and storing basic foods, fallout shelter construction, weapons for defense, and much more.

5. **Skills for Survival** by Esther Dickey, Horizon Publishing, 1978, $14.95. This book covers the basic necessities for times of hardship: emergency clothing, water distillation, emergency fallout shelters, & food storage. Also excellent gardening guide on how to extend growing seasons.

6. **Survive Safely Anywhere** by John Wiseman, Crown Publishing, 1986, $16.95. Written by an ex-SAS survival trainer, this manual is one of the best on outdoors survival.

7. **The Best of Woodsmoke** edited by Richard L. Jamison, Horizon Publishing, 1982, $16.95 Articles by eleven authors on the best ways to live off the land. This is a must!!!

8. **NITRO-PACK Catalog**. This is the best mailorder source of preparedness items in terms of quality and availability. We recommend them highly! $3.00, see our order blank (good toward your first purchase)

Surviving Global Slavery

Rodale Publishing/Yankee Magazine's Forgotten Arts Collection

9. **Forgotten Arts 1**: Managing a woodlot; cooking on a wood stove; keeping a family cow; cooking wild greens; keeping chickens; whole-wheat bread from grain to loaf; drying beans and corn; natural dyes; apple cider and vinegar; making soap. $6.95

10. **Forgotten Arts 2**: Digging a well; making paint from scratch; making a ladder; keeping sheep; building a smokehouse; coping with a whole pig; old-fasion stenciling; simple wooden toys; fireplace cookery; keeping geese, guinea hens, & peacocks. $6.95

11. **Forgotten Arts 3**: Portable fences; drying flowers; building a grape arbor; weaving baskets; painting patterned floors; working with a draft horse; reclaiming an apple tree; sharpening tools; making bricks; root cellars. $6.95

12. **Forgotten Arts 4**: Making ice cream; selecting a wood stove; reclaiming garden soil; making maple syrup; drying fruits and vegetables; growing flax; medicinal herbs; building bridges; constructing rual driveways; building a skating rink. $6.95

13. **Forgotten Arts 5**: Tape loom weaving; pickling meats and vegetables; reseating chairs; laying a slate roof; making a hammock; clock repairing; caring for quilts; splicing rope; reclaiming an overgrown field. $6.95

Home Storage

14. **Beginner's Guide to Family Preparedness** by Rosalie Mason, Horizon Publishers, 1977, $10.95. An excellent book for those just starting out in food storage and other preparedness subjects.

15. **The New Seed Starters Handbook** by Nancy Bubel, Rodale Press, 1988, $14.95. When to start seeds, what depth to plant them, how to water them, what type of light is best, how to protect seedlings, and much more is here in this complete guide, written by a veteran gardener, to starting more than 200 plants from seed.

16. **Square Foot Gardening** by Mel Bartholomew, Rodale Press, 1981, $14.95. We can't say enough about this book. It is the best approach to intensive gardening!!! It sounds crazy but much less work equals higher yields. One fifth the space and work of a conventional row garden.

17. **Fool Proof Planting** by Anne Moyer Halpin, Rodale Press, 1990, $14.95. The ultimate in planting guides for seed starting, grafting, budding, layering, rooting stem cuttings, and root division.

18. **Home Garden Hints** by Alan K. Briscoe, Horizon Publishing, $3.95. Helpful hints are offered on insects and disease control, compost, mulching, and companion planting, starting transplants, how and when to fertilize, and much more.

19. **Rodale Book of Composting** edited by Deborah L. Martin and Grace Gershuny, Rodale

Press, 1992, $14.95 The ultimate composting book, this title even goes into how to compost in urban environments, neighborhood projects, and at home. Includes plans for different compost bins and a variety of techniques and methods.

20. **Farmers of Forty Centuries** by F.H. King, Rodale Press, 1911, $17.95. Permanent agriculture in China, Korea, and Japan. Covers how the farmers in these countries have traditionally handled: intensive cultivation, composting, crop rotation, green manuring, intertillage, and irrigation. What would be survival to us is business as usual to them.

21. **Saving Seeds** by Marc Rogers, Storey/Garden Way Publishing, $9.95. The gardener's guide to growing and storing vegetable and flower seeds. Preserves non-hybrids and saves money.

22. **Rodale's All New Encyclopedia of Organic Gardening** edited by Fern Marshall Bradley and Barbara W. Ellis, Rodale Press, 1992, $29.95. A treasure trove of organic gardening facts, this is the best book on all aspects of organic gardening available. "Why organic?", you ask. Because we may not always have petro-chemical based fertilizers and bug sprays.

23. **Stocking Up III** by Carol Hupping, Rodale Press, 1986, $24.95. This is the best book on canning food available.

24. **The ABC's of Home Food Dehydration** by Barbara Densley, Horizon Publishing, 1975, $7.95.

Home Storage

Basic guide to all kinds of food dehydration. Includes selecting a home dehydrator, the drying process, pretratment of food, rehydration of food, numerous recipes and helpful tips.

25. **Home Food Dehydrating** by Jay and Shirley Bills, Horizon Publishing, 1974, $9.95. An excellent all-round beginner's book on the dehydration of foods.

26. **New Concepts In Dehydrated Food Cookery** by Barbara Densley, Horizon Publishing, 1982, $12.95. This book teaches how to incorporate the reconstitution and cooking of dehytdrated foods into your regular menu. It's also excellent as an update on the latest in dehydration theory.

27. **Root Cellaring** by Mike and Nancy Bubel, Storey Publishing, $12.95. The simple, no-cost no-processing way to store your garden's bounty. This storage method which requires little work, no canning jars or freezer bags, and no fuel makes a lot of sense. A cold storage area can be created almost anywhere, even in a closet.

28. **The Home Water Source** by Stu Campbell, Storey Publishing, $16.96. How to find, filter, store, and conserve a home water source.

29. **Fun With Fruit Preservation** by Dora D. Flack, Horizon Publishing, 1980, $7.95. Detailed coverage on all aspects of fruit preservation: fruit leather, drying, dehydrating, canning, bottling. Notes on jams, jellies, juices, and syrups. Includes freezing, basement storage, as well as out build-

ings, root cellars, and pits.

30. **Cheese Making Made Easy** by Ricki and Robert Carroll, Storey Publish, $9.95. Sixty delicious varieties, easy to follow recipes.

31. **Jellies & Jams**, Rodale Press, $6.95. A forgotten Art book, this is all you'll ever need to learn how to make these mouth-watering condiments.

32. **Pickles & Relishes**, Rodale Press, $6.95. Same as HS-9 above but for pickles and relishes of all kinds.

33. **Basic Butchering of Livestock and Game** by John J. Mettler Jr., DVM, Storey Publishing, $11.95. An excellent how-to for beef, veal, hogs, lamb, and poultry.

34. **Bee Prepared with Honey** by Arthur W. Andersen, Horizon Publishing, 1975, $9.95. Shows the nutritianal value of honey, provides 140 recipes using honey, and teaches basic backyard bee keeping.

35. **Practical Beekeeping** by Enoch Tompkins and Roger Griffith, Storey Publishing, $9.95. An excellent primer on bee keeping for beginners.

36. **Hive Management** by Richard Bonney, Storey Publishing, $14.95. More advanced, concentrates on the scheduling of bee work.

37. **Chickens in your Backyard** by Rick and Gail Luttmann, Rodale Press, 1976, $9.95. A

beginner's guide aimed at small backyard or sub-urban conditions.

38. **Ducks and Geese in your Backyard** by Rick and Gail Luttmann, Rodale Press, 1978, $9.95. Learn how to shop for birds and how to raise flock from eggs.

39. **Raising Poultry the Modern Way** by Leonard S. Mercia, Storey Publishing, $9.95. Detailed info, all you need to know.

40. **Keeping Livestock Healthy** by N. Bruce Haynes, DVM, Storey Publishing, $14.95. A good, basic veterinary guide.

41. **The Family Cow** by Dirk Van Loon, Storey Publishing, 1976, $12.95. Super guide to cows and their history.

42. **Raising a Calf for Beef** by Phyllis Hobson, Storey Publishing, $7.95. This book concentrates on the beef calf, as opposed to the milk cow.

43. **Raising Milk Goats the Modern Way** by Jerry Belanger, Storey Publishing, 1975, $9.95. A good basic manual on dairy goats.

44. **Raising Sheep the Modern Way** by Paula Simmons, Storey Publishing, $9.95. A good basic manual on sheep raising.

45. **Turning Wool into a Cottage Industry** by Paula Simmons, Storey Publishing, $14.95. How to make a living with wool and how to use it for

survival means.

46. Small Scale Pig Raising by Dirk Van Loon, Storey Publishing, $12.95. All you really need to know to bring home the bacon.

47. A Veterinary Guide for Animal Owners by C.E. Spaulding, DVM, Rodale Press, 1976, $17.95. Excellent reference book. Includes prevention and cures of many animal diseases.

48. Laurel's Kitchen Bread Book by Laurel Robertson and others, Ten-Speed Press, $18.00. An excellent bread-making manual by one of the nation's to vegetarian writer.

49. Doin' Dutch Oven Inside by Robert L. Ririe, Horizon Publishing, 1990, $8.95. Dutch oven cast iron cookware is one of the best ways to cook. This book tells how to use this cookware in the house as well as outdoors.

50. Allied Cast Iron Cookware & Accessories Catalog, The best source for dutch oven cookware. Order through our mailorder service in the back of this book. $1.00.

51. Dutch Oven Secrets by Lynn Hopkins, Horizon Publishing, 1990, $8.95. A manual on the care, seasoning, cleaning, and storing of dutch oven cookware.

52. Lets Cook Dutch by Robert L. Ririe, Horizon Publishing, 1979, $7.95. A treasure trove of dutch oven recipes.

53. **Dry Peas and Lentils** by Betty Lowe Janson, Horizon Publishing, 1990, $14.95. An excellent guide to cooking with complete vegetable proteins. Many inexpensive yet healthy, tasty recipes.

54. **The Enchanted Broccoli Forest** by Mollie Katzen, Ten-Speed Press, $16.95. Excellent vegetarian recipes for those times when meat may not be in abundance.

55. **Just Add Water** by Barbara G. Salsbury, Horizon Publishing, 1972, $6.95. How to use dehydrated foods and meat substitutes. It is considered a classic.

56. **New Recipes From Moose Wood** by Moosewood Collective, Ten-Speed Press, $13.95. Another excellent set of recipes from the author of the Enchanted Broccoli Forest.

57. **Cooking Home Storage** by Peggy Layton and Vicki Tate, $12.95. How to make the best of those cheap, easy to store staples such as grains and beans. Even the kids will like these. Includes how much and what to store.

58. **Lehman's Non-Electric Catalog**, When I first saw this catalog which services the Amish and Menonite communities, it was like strolling back through time. This is the greatest collection of hand tools and accessories for self-reliant homesteading I have ever seen. We used many of the items they offer in the operation of my grandfather's

farm in Indiana. Order through our mail order section. $2.00.

59. **Abundant Life Seeds Catalog,** The best source of heirloom seeds I know. These are original strains of garden vegetables and grains. They will breed true year after year. Order though our mail order section for $1.00.

60. **Native Seeds / Search.** Excellent for Southwestern and Western growing climes. They carry many native-American heirloom food seeds. Drought resistant & hardy. $1.00

CHAPTER 6
RELIGION

Those who know them say the individuals behind the globalist movement are apolitical and amoral. They have no interest in Judeo-Christian values. However, this doesn't mean they don't appreciate the usefulness of religion as a tool for control. It is not surprising they have chosen to establish relationships with the New Age movement. In many cases, they have supplied significant monetary support to this quasi-religious system. Some of the strangest cultic figure heads have received funds to form various foundations dedicated to world-wide peace movements, world-wide governments, world-wide meditation efforts, save-the-planet actions, transformational management schools, etc..

What is the New Age Movement (NAM)? It is a wide range of occult practices. Randall N. Baer, a former top New Age Movement leader who finally found Christ, describes what the NAM is all about in his book, [1] **Inside the New Age Nightmare**.

"What is the New Age Movement? Essentially, it is a Satan controlled, modern-day mass revival of occult-based philosophies and practices in both obvious and cleverly disguised forms. In effect, it is an end-times plague of the spirit, propagating the powerful delusion that they should believe the lie. It is nothing more than a glitteringly seductive, broad road leading only to eventual destruction. The New Age is actually not anything new at all. It always has been active throughout history in numerous and widespread Western occult traditions and Eastern mystical religions. Over the last three decades, however, an enormous and unprecedented massive revival of occult-based practices has been taking place, some of it disguised as being non-occult in nature. To many peoples' surprise, New Age philosophy and practices have crept into the very fabric of American society in both subtle and profound ways. The magnitude and momentum of this movement is to such an extent that it poses one of the fastest-growing threats to Christianity today, especially in the years ahead as the endtimes unfold. What do most people think of when they hear the term New Age? Shirley MacLaine? Harmonic Convergence? Reincarnation? Crystal power? Channeling? Psychic readers? In fact these are only a part of a very broad spectrum of different New Age forms, strategies, and practices. To make matters all the more difficult, the term New Age is sometimes not even used, when something is actually New Age at the core."[p.78-79]

As Mr. Baer states, New Age philosophy is not new. There was a significant upsurge of NAM practices in Europe just before Hitler's rise to power. It set the stage for his acceptance by the German people as an occult Messiah. Today we live under similar dangers.

Mr. Baer says: "In effect, The New Age is one of several major gateways for the adversary to unleash his plans and forces for global domination. The Antichrist comes bearing an innovative orthodox science in one hand and a Universal Oneness (neo-New Age) philosophy in the other, seated on a politico-economic throne of worldly power. A One-World Order, headed by the ultimate wolf in sheep's clothing, offers a desperate world many miracles, gifts,and wonders in the name of peace, love, planetary healing and universal brotherhood." [p.83]

A True Danger

Some of you may be saying, "So what? If I live a good Christian life, nothing will happen to me!" Don't be too sure! New Age publications have lately been damning Christians for holding back the world's transition into an enlightened age. John Ankerberg and John Weldon point out in their book, [2] **The Facts on the New Age Movement**:

"A thorough reading of New Age literature will show that some New Agers sanction the persecution of Christians. They do so on the basis of the need to remove those who may refuse to accept or attempt to prevent a spiritual uniting of humanity."

"This is one of the darker aspects of the New Age, yet it is consistent with the overall world of the NAM. If true globalism— or world unity — is eventually to be a reality, then by definition all dissenting voices must either be converted, silenced, or removed. That, of course, is the rub,— the NewAge of love and harmony may have to be repressive for a time to usher in their version of peace on Earth."

Troy Lawrence says in his fascinating book, [3] **New Age Messiah Identified**, "Like the Jews, fundamentalists and Evangelical Christians exist in every nation in the world. The New World Order would have to be just that— international, if they were to gather the Christians for a free trip to spirit realms. If the United Nations, controlled by the New Group of World Servers, had control of all the nuclear arsenal, then it could force every nation to 'deliver up' the Christians. Many professing Christ will, no doubt, bend the knee to Baal. The true Evangelical and fundamentalist christians will be fewer than what is counted now— the threat of death will assure that. Those that do not receive the mark will be 'marked' for extinction. Nations that refuse to deliver up the Christians will be threatened with nuclear annihilation. [p. 179]"

Strategies

"How do we deal with this?", you ask. "Aren't we supposed to turn the other cheek?"

Yes, that is correct. It is important to

Religion

understand that many New Agers have no idea of the full ramifications of their efforts to "enlighten" us poor Christians. They may smile at us tenderly as they ship us off to "re-education camps", thinking they are doing us a great favor. These people have been misled. If you find yourselves in this kind of situation, hold fast to the Gospel! Reject their attempts to convert or brainwash you. Remember, the Vietnam War POWs who served the longest years yet kept their sanity were the ones who had a strong grounding in the Gospel of our Lord, Jesus Christ.

How should you act on the outside, living in a society where all are required to accept the mark of the beast?— like a sheep in wolves' country. Try not to draw attention to yourselves. Before the tribulations are over, good Christians may find themselves hiding out from persecution. There may yet be another "underground railroad". The saints may find themselves traveling clandestinely to enclaves of safety. Some have said that in the last days, the Rocky mountains will be a refuge to the Saints. We may see the United States split up into factions, immersed in civil war. Some of those areas may be friendly to Christians and some may not be.

Don't despair, it's possible to ready yourselves now for these times. In addition to a good storage program, you should plan on being able to move over land to safety. If fuel is not available, you should plan on animal or human-powered transportation. You may have to practice escape and evasion to get to safety. There are a number

Surviving Global Slavery

of excellent publications available which teach how best to do this (see the Chapter 5 resource section).

Although it is possible for a family unit to plan and practice for such times, there is greater safety in numbers. Share this with your Church or your Scriptures-study group. Start preparing as a group of friends and neighbors to help one another. A Neighborhood-Watch program would be a perfect start toward neighborhood unity. Expand upon that structure. Develop emergency action plans for future contingencies. Be prepared to take care of one another.

Use the talents of those friends and relatives who have military planning experience.

The Critical Aspect

The most important preparatory work you can do is in the Spiritual realm. First pray often, with real intent. Second, devote at least fifteen minutes or more a day to scriptural study. Third, try to live a Christ-like life. Always be ready to help and forgive others. Fourth, instill these attitudes in your families. Five, learn to depend on Christ. Exercise your faith in the Lord. Faith is like a muscle, if you don't use it, you may lose it. Get yourselves right with God!

Imagine how tough it will be to practice Christianity under the New World Order. Role play how you should react to trying situations with your family. Establish networks with fellow

Religion

Christians of like-minds. Remember, the really bad times will only last three-and-a-half years. Think about what may happen during that time and plan for all possibilities.

You may be asked to die for your faith if you reject the mark of the beast. Are you spiritually prepared to do that? Are you prepared to see your loved ones tortured or killed for a religious principle? Are you spiritually, emotionally, and physically strong enough to travel great distances through hostile territory to attain safety? I think you can see why it is important to begin preparations now for the coming bad times. **Please remember, the spiritual preparations are the most important ones!**

RESOURCES

1. **Inside the New Age Nightmare** by Randall N. Baer, Huntington House, 1989.

2. **The Facts on the New Age Movement** by John Ankerburg & John Weldon, Harvest Publishers, 1988.

3. **New Age Messiah Identified** by Troy Lawrence, Huntington House, 1991.

Surviving Global Slavery

CHAPTER 7
EDUCATION

Those who advocate the New World Order see our education system as one of the primary means to an end— the destruction of families and the creation of willing consumer subjects. Even if they were to allow the children of those people who refuse the mark of the beast to go to public schools, you might not like what your children would learn there.

To gain a better understanding of the type of education being offered in the schools of the future, we need only examine the platform of the National Educators Association, the NEA. According to Samuel L. Blumenfeld in his book, [1] **NEA: Trojan Horse in American Education**, this Super-union of teachers and other education specialists has a powerful political agenda. Its so unfortunate that teachers at the local level are more or less forced to become members of the NEA, because most do not agree with all the aspects of this agenda. Many are not even aware of what their organization's national-level officers and special interest groups are proposing. The following six points are taken from their 1990 National Convention's goals:

1. Get all children into public pre-schools by the

Surviving Global Slavery

age of three. Make kindergarten compulsory.

The quicker these people can separate children from their parents, the quicker and more thoroughly can they be programed for the purposes of the globalists.

2. Begin psychiatric experimentation at the prekindergarten level.

If our children's vulnerabilities and compulsions can be identified early on, it will be much easier to program and control them. Again, this is a control enhancer.

3. Provide sexuality classes for all grades and distribute contraceptives to minors without parental knowledge or consent.

There are groups who desire a totally responsibility-free sexual lifestyle. They are not interested in controlled sex, but in promiscuous lifestyles. They recognize a certain percentage of all youth will grow up to be homosexual adults. They want to insure that this percentage, or "their kind" will be allowed to attain the same sexual orientations as their own. In fact, they would like to see as many youth as possible co-opted into the Gay life. This would mean that many more potential playmates for the present adult homosexual population. These sexuality classes do not teach abstinence and monogamy. Rather, they urge "safe sex" and plenty of it. This graphically illustrates the hold Satan has on these poor, lost souls.
4. Totally oppose home schooling, parental choice

110

in education, tuition tax credits, education vouchers, and parental supervision of schools.

The fact that home-schooled children generally score much higher on the SAT test, that they spend less hours per day in structured lessons yet are ready for promotion to higher levels of difficulty much sooner than their public school peers has the NEA scared. Their great deception of the American public becomes transparent when facts like these come to light. It's no surprize to us that public schools are failing to provide the most basic education to a large percentage of our children. How serious is the NEA's opposition? Last year the Missouri NEA Chapter met in Kansas City and set aside $7-million to fight home schooling. That is a significant war chest for one state-wide organization!

Their opposition to the other educational free-choice aspects indicate their concern about an exodus from public classrooms. Their jobs are at stake, as are their professional reputations.

5. Unwed student mothers should receive tax-payer funded abortions on demand throughout any of the nine months of pregnancy.

The reason may be given that this will insure young ladies will remain in school, if they become pregnant. It will also encourage promiscuity, not to mention the murder of the unwanted babies. The NEA won't address these issues, of course.

Surviving Global Slavery

6. Homosexuals should be allowed to teach in the classrooms, even if they have AIDS. They should also be allowed to work as student counselors.

Do we want these kinds of role models? Can they be trusted to provide good advice to their charges? One shudders to imagine the Pandora's box this would open.

STRATEGIES

The obvious solutions are:

- Home schooling
- Co-op Church or neighborhood home schooling

RESOURCES

1. **NEA: Trojan Horse in American Education** by Samuel L. Blumenfeld, Paradigm, 1984, $9.95.

2. **The Big Book of Home Learning** by Mary Pride, $69.00. This is a huge, 4-volume set broken out by I Starting Out ($15), II Primary/Elementary ($19.50), III Teens/Adolescents ($15), IV After ($15). All home schoolers say these are the best source books available.

3. **Home Education Magazine**, $20 a year, P.O. Box 1083, Dept UFD, Tonasket, WA 98855.

4. **Home Sweet Home**, $20 4xs a year, E. 201 Bourgault, Dept UFD, Shelton, WA 98584.

112

CHAPTER 8
MEDICAL CONCERNS

This area is probably the toughest to compensate for. Even today, increasing numbers of people are being locked out of professional health care. Costs have driven up insurance policy prices until companies can only afford the cheapest, most basic plans or none at all. In an attempt to make up the deficit, liberals in Congress are currently attempting to inaugurate legislation which would require business to contribute to insurance programs— either private or government sponsored. Many Mom and Pop small businesses will most likely be forced to close their doors. This will further exacerbate our economic problems.

Formal medical treatment will not be available to those who do not accept the mark. Hopefully there will be a few doctors who will be good Christians. They may be willing to provide basic care for barter arrangement or out of the goodness of their hearts. Prescription drugs will not be available, however. Many will have to rely on herbal medicines and homopathic medical practices. Although certainly more primitive, this alternative can be effective. The major loss of service, outside of prescription drugs, will be high

113

tech diagnostic testing facilities. We won't have the ability to know what's wrong with us.

In general, our quality of life will be significantly degraded. But remember, it's only for three and a half years. Now's the time to get yourselves squared away as much as possible. For example, one of my daughters required minor surgery early last year. I had both knees operated on in May of last year. These procedures maxed out my contribution share to my medical plan. Everything beyond that was 100% paid for by the insurance company. We took advantage of this situation to take care of several other problems in the family. I had operations on both hands to alleviate some carpal tunnel syndrome problems. One side on my nose had closed off from old wrestling injuries. As a result, every time I flew (which is often), I got an ear infection. Rebreaking the nose and reaming out the sinuses took care of this problem. My two youngest daughters had their tonsils out, and my wife had some preventative diagnostic tests done, since her mother had died early due to cancer. The whole family went for the gusto, knowing we would never have another chance to take care of so many needs so cheaply. We joke about 1991 being the year of "Bionic Bob"; however, we feel much more confident about facing the tribulations.

If you have long-standing medical conditions which should be fixed, you might want to stop putting them off. Now is the time to get them fixed, not after you've rejected the mark of the beast.

Medical Concerns

STRATEGIES

In addition to taking care of your medical problems as soon as possible, it's time to begin stockpiling medical supplies. Every time you buy a cold remedy, buy two or three times as much as you usually do. The same goes for any other over-the-counter drugs, bandages, etc. For those medicines requiring prescriptions, there is a way of accumulating them. In Chapter 2, I mentioned how I was able to stockpile the anti-irritant medicine I take for my knees. This method, however, won't work for antibiotics.

One is supposed to take an entire "series", usually ten days from start to finish. The only time this won't happen is when an antibiotic is not working for a particular problem. Doctors will sometimes stop a patient in the middle of a series to change him over to a different one. If that happens to you, save the unused portion for your medical stockpile. Be sure to check with your pharmacist about storage life and any potential problems. Some medicines lose their punch or change chemically over long periods of time. Only an expert can tell you which ones will and what can result from taking them.

Homopathic Medicine

Another strategy is to become familiar with herbal and other forms of natural medicine. This is called homopathic medicine. The Chinese have been very good at this for several thousand years.

Surviving Global Slavery

Although Westerners will find their medical theory different from what most of us believe, their herbal cures are generally excellent.

We Westerners have our herbal medicines as well. the best book I know on medicinal herbs found in the U.S. is, [1] **From the Shepherd's Purse**. This superb work presents numerous herbs, grouped in medicinal groups. Each herb is shown in a color photo, surrounded by its natural environment. This is helpful for finding it in its natural state in the wild. A detailed line drawing of the complete plant, roots and all, points out what parts of the plant are used for what purposes. It is not unusual to find multiple uses out of one plant. Detailed descriptions then go into where the herb is normally found, what time of day and season and how it should be harvested, and how each usable part should be prepared and administered for what illnesses. I know of no better work on this subject.

Later on, we plan to put together a computer program which will allow the user to select their symptoms. The computer will then provide alternative home remedy possibilities and the appropriate herbal drug dosages. For those of you who get on our mailing list, we will let you know just as soon as it's published.

Training

It would be advisable for family members to become skilled in first aid. Several excellent programs exist, the Scouts and Red Cross to name a couple. Many communities teach their

Medical Concerns

own. Some community colleges teach an Emergency Medical Technician course and nursing courses. A mid-wife course might prove helpful. There are also a number of commercial programs which go more into combat medicine. One of these is the **Infinity Self-Reliance Center** in Harrisburg, Missouri. Check your local Yellow Pages and the ads in survival magazines for other training sources.

RESOURCES

1. **From the Shepherd's Purse** by Max G. Barlow, Spice West Publications, 1990, $26.00. It doesn't get any better than this! Each herb is shown in its natural state in a color photo. Detailed line drawings then show which part is good for what ailment. Information includes where, whem, and how to pick and prepare.

2. **The Healing Herbs** by Michael Castleman, Rodale Press, 1991, $27.95. Goes beyond plants to symptoms, conditions, the dangers of side effects and overdose.

3. **Rodale's Illustrated Encyclopedia of Herbs** edited by Claire Kowalchik & William H. Hylton, Rodale Press, 1987, $24.95 Everything on how to

Surviving Global Slavery

CHAPTER 9
TRANSPORTATION

By rejecting the mark of the beast, you may find it difficult to legally drive a motor vehicle. You won't be able to pay personal property tax or registration fees. In addition, it is difficult to store POL products for a long time. It will be challenging to support and maintain your vehicles. How should you cope with this lack of traditional transportation? There are three viable overland transportation options available:

- Hand carts
- Draft-animal carts and sleds
- Bicycles
- Horseback

HAND CARTS

In the 1830/40 time frame, some of our pioneer ancestors were too poor to afford wagons and draft animals. They were forced to cross the plains and mountains with all they owned in hand carts. These were generally two-wheeled conveyances with drawing bars or handles in the front. It's easier to pull than it is to push a great weight.

119

Its also easier to guide such a cart from the front. Today, there are a number of commercially built garden carts which make use of a box-like contraption mounted on an axle with two balloon tired bicycle wheels, and a "U"-shaped handle.

It would not be too difficult to handcraft a larger version of this cart. These commercial versions are probably not large enough for our purposes.

DRAFT-ANIMAL CARTS

Smaller carts, using four bicycle wheels, could be hooked to large dogs. This has been done for centuries in Europe. Most dog books which describe the different breeds will tell which ones have been used for this type of work in the past. Obviously, it will take some lead-time to train your animal(s). The dog breeds traditionally used as cart or sled dogs are: the Siberian Huskey, the Samoyed, the Alaskan Malamute, the Eskimo or Greenland dog, and the Bernese mountain dog.

A larger horse or cow-drawn wagon could be made from an old pickup truck long-bed and axle with two tires. A 4x4 should be bolted onto the frame underneath and extended forward 8-10 feet as a wagon tongue. It might not be a bad idea to take a family vacation to one of the Amish or Mennonite communities to see how they do these things. In Ohio and Pennsylvania it is possible to purchase a number of horse-drawn conveyances from Amish factories.

Transportation

Draft horses are still being bred. One of the best places to look for breeder addresses is in [1] **The Draft Horse Journal**. The following breeds have traditionally been used as draft animals: Belgium, Clydesdale, Perchenon, and Suffolk.

BICYCLES

The bicycle is one of the most versatile means of transportation man has ever used. Back in the early 1970's, I saw Koreans haul the most incredible loads on the backs of bikes: heavy grain sacks full of rice (220 lbs), ten-feet-high stacks of goods, and long reinforcing steel bars. One of the funniest incidents I witnessed in Korea involved a farmer, a pig, and a bicycle. The farmer had a rather large sow he needed to take to market. He built a plywood platform onto the back of his bike to accommodate her body. He then fed her full of homebrew beer mash until she passed out. He and several of his neighbors manhandled her unconscious bulk onto the platform and tied her on with rubber cords.

The farmer took off for market, peddling like mad. Unfortunately, he either wasn't fast enough or he misjudged the power of the beer mash sleeping draught. Half way to market on the main highway, the sow awoke. She was not a happy camper. As her frantic struggles grew greater and greater, the farmer's eyes got bigger and bigger. The bike started wandering all over the road like it had a mind of its own. The pig's screams grew louder and louder. All cars passing by were in danger of driving into the ditch or each

Surviving Global Slavery

other. Pedestrians within sight and sound started choking with laughter and falling all over themselves.

From personal experience, I have found thin-tired 10-speed bicycles are too fragile for survival purposes. The heavy-framed, thick-tired mountain bikes are much more practical for long distance trips, cross-country movement, and burden carriers. One interesting possible use of the bike for transporting bulky or heavy loads is to build a wooden framework with a platform between two bikes. If you brace them together at the tops and bottoms of both bikes, it should be very stable. I recommend ganging the two handlebars together so if one turns, the other will also. It's possible for one person to ride one bike and steer both in this manner.

HORSEBACK

In addition to draft horse load pulling, there is the possibility of transporting people on horseback and load bearing by pack horses. An excellent book on how to make and pack packframes is listed in the resource section.

RESOURCES

1. **The Draft Horse Journal**, P.O. Box 670, Waverly, IA 50677, $16.00 per year quarterly.

2. **Packing**, Northland Publishing, 1989, $11.95. The ultimate source book on how to use pack animals.

CHAPTER 10
GETTING OFF THE POWER GRID

If you don't accept the mark of the beast, how will you pay the utility bills? Most of us have taken for granted the convenience of electricity, gas, sewage, and water service to our homes. Without the mark, we will have to either go back to very primitive conditions or go forward to high technology solutions. This chapter takes the more positive view of the high tech approach.

Getting off the grid is not cheap, but it is possible. These technologies have improved tremendously over the past ten years. Let us examine the options for power generation and storage, water, and sewage treatment. Unfortunately we may have to do without natural gas.

Power Generation and Storage

There are two primary means of home power generation: one is wind power and the other is sun power. Both depend on the functions of where you live and your weather patterns. Water power is another viable option, but only if you live near your own running water.

• **Wind Power**. Windmills have come a long way from wind- powered water pumps out on the range. Wind turbines have come into their own. Here in Kansas there are people who generate enough electricity to sell all excess to their personal needs to the power company. The turbine unit usually goes on top of a steel tower similar to a ham radio operator's— usually 60-100 feet above the ground. The unit is designed to govern its own speed to prevent damage in high winds and gusts. The power it generates goes through a control unit and then into a battery storage unit or directly into the house.

The advantage of using a battery-based electrical unit is continuity of power when the wind falls off. The advantage of going directly into the house system is that it can be metered by the power company. If the latter method is used, the power company will install a meter which can go backwards or forward. If you use more power than you generate, the meter goes forward and you pay the power company regular retail prices for the power used. If you generate more power than you use, the meter runs backward and the company buys the excess power off you at wholesale prices. Your system must, however, have an automatic cut-off switch which will cut the wind generated power off the grid immediately if the grid loses power. The last thing a lineman or sub-station maintenance man needs is to begin working on a supposedly dead circuit, only to find your generated power on it. This could ruin his whole day.

Getting Off The Power Grid

Using the wind to charge a battery-bank is a good way to cut off the electrical grid system entirely. Some homesteaders use a combination of wind and sun power generation to insure a plenitude of regeneration. After the sun goes down, the wind continues to provide power. A typical 1500W wind system may cost around $4,500 to $5,500 for the turbine, the tower, and the control unit. A more typical home-unit of 10 Kilowatts may cost as much as $24,000. As I said earlier, its not cheap to get off the power grid.

• **Sun Power**. The technical term for this kind of power is photovoltaic. The sun light strikes panels of photoelectric cells which turn the sun's energy into electricity. Often the panels are mounted on special racks which track the sun (sort of like sun flowers). The power then goes through a charge controller and a direct current load center into a battery bank. Then it goes through an inverter which produces alternating current and 110/220 voltages. Again, all this is not cheap. You may spend from $5,000 to $25,000 for a photovoltaic system.

Water

This may become a real problem in urban areas. Actually, it may become a real problem anywhere. So much of our ground water has become dangerously polluted. If you do not have the situation or the wherewithal to drill your own well, you may have to rely on barter with someone

125

who does. Storing a four-year's supply of water purification supplies is an essential consideration.

Sewage

This is actually a benefit more than it is a problem. The answer is a composting toilet. Costing about $1,200, this device desiccates human waste and makes it fit for garden use. They install right in the bathroom or basement and require venting but no plumbing.

The second solution is to build an outhouse. They're stinky, but they work.

RESOURCES

1. The best source of products and information on these areas of concern is a company called Real Goods Trading Corp., 966 Mazzoni St, Ukiah, CA 95482.   Their excellent **Alternative Energy Sourcebook** is available through our mail order service for $16.00.

2.   **Home Power Magazine**, P.O. Box 130, Hornbrook, CA 96044-0130, (916) 475-3179, $10.00 a year, bi-monthly. This publication is filled with articles by people who are off the grid and doing it sucessfully. The magazine is somewhat technical but so is the subject.

CHAPTER 11
LAW AND SELF DEFENSE

If the New World Order takes over the planet, expect changes in the way the business of laws and law enforcement is done. As indicated in Chapter 1, there will be laws and regulations overseen by agencies governing everything about our lives. If you think government is too big now, just wait. You ain't seen nothin' yet!

State Department papers indicate all privately owned weapons will be confiscated. The only people with weapons will be "Peace Keeping" forces and "Internal Security" forces. That's a rather chilling substitution for the word "policemen"— internal security forces.

If you want to research what life may be like in the near future, look up everything you can on the Federal Emergency Management Act and Agency or FEMA. This act, its related executive orders, and its agency's contingency plans are already in place. In the event of a national emergency, such as an attack on the government, widespread natural disasters, or such disruptions as a total collapse of the banking system, a state of emergency will be announced and FEMA will kick in. At this point, our country becomes a police state. One executive order will direct all Postmasters to register and I.D. all people living within their respective jurisdictions. Another will direct the local law enforcement agencies to confiscate all privately owned weapons. Another will direct the formation of work brigades under the aegis of a program named the Citizens Skills Acquisition program.

How about those who disagree with the overturning of our constitution? Provisions have already been made for any dissenters. Currently National Guard, Border Patrol, and other enforcement agencies have stockpiled the materiels and supplies for concentration camps to be set up throughout our country. Shades of American-Japanese internment in WWII— these camps are designed to hold up to 12,000 personnel. Families will be forcibly split up. It is thought that men will work harder if they are not distracted by their families nearby.

If all this doesn't scare you, consider the probable breakdown in society during the transition. There will be those who go along with this peacefully, others may break out there guns and seek to conduct guerrilla action against the encroaching tyranny, and there will be criminal elements who will decide to grab whatever they can while the grabbing is good. Christians and Jews will be persecuted as scapegoats during all this.

Law and Self Defense

DEFENSE STRATEGIES

What is there to do about all this? How can one make it through these times? This is a significant moral dilemma. Most of us who have ever raised our hands and swore to defend the constitution against all enemies, foreign or domestic, instinctively feel like we should be taking some kind of action. On the other hand, it is elements within our own government who, under the influence, manipulation, or direction of the New World Order elitists, are suborning the constitution. Are we supposed to defend the government, right or wrong? Or, should we defend the constitution? Or, should we do nothing?

First, I think its important to not give up on political activism until the bitter end. If, despite our best efforts, the New World Order comes about. We need to be ready for those times.

The best attitude to take is one which Christ called, "Going as a sheep in wolves' country". If you want to increase your chances of surviving, don't be an active tax protester or anything else which gets you identified as a "trouble-maker". Keep a low profile, don't break laws, and don't come on as a threat to the Globalists.

"What about you, Mr. Spear? Here you are writing a book against the Globalists. Aren't you afraid you'll be at jeopardy?"

Yes, I've probably placed myself at risk; however, I would rather face the Globalists and all they might dream up to do to me than to face the Lord at Judgement and explain why I didn't pass on what I know to help my Brothers and Sisters through the Tribulations. I'm willing to take my chances. The worst they can do is to kill me and mine. They can only get my body, not my soul.

SELF DEFENSE

You run your most dangerous personal risks during the transition into the New World Order. There may civil uprisings with looting, raping, etc. All able bodied members of your family should know the basics of self defense. They should be able to defend themselves and one another with guns, knives, or clubs, as well as with their bare hands.

"This is not a Christian attitude," you say. I don't believe Christ meant for us not to defend ourselves. I think he meant for us not to take revenge, which can shrivel one's soul. We have protected our country in war. We have protected our citizens on the streets. I believe it's ok to protect our own if society breaks down.

To learn how to do so, see the resource section for our best training resources.

RESOURCES

The following are all books on personal security

Law and Self Defense

and defense by the author.

1. Survival On The Battlefield— A Handbook to Military Martial Arts: A Military Book Club selection, this book has sold all over the world. Special Forces units have used it as a training manual. There is material in here found in no other publication. The essence of dealing harshly with a battlefield enemy! $14.95

2. Close Quarters Combat for Police and Security Forces: Numerous controlling and containment techniques for unarmed and nightstick bearing personnel. Complete training program. $19.95

1 & 2. Combination: The ultimate fighting system contained in the two above books provides many options to fit with wide-ranging threats. $30.00 special price

3. Surviving Hostage Situations: Written for families and lay-personnel, this book has been used to train volunteer workers at the Kansas State Prison. It sells all over the world and has been translated into German. It covers all aspects of hostage taking and gives strategies on how to deal with criminal, prison, and terrorist situations. $14.95

4. Hapkido— The Integrated Fighting Art: Said to be the ultimate street art, Hapkido is based on the combination of the ancient Korean art of Taek Yeong and Japanese Jujitsu. This overview

Surviving Global Slavery

of the art was written by Robert K. Spear, 6th dan black belt and Chairman of the U.S. Hapkido Federation's Examination Board. $12.95

5. Military Knife Fighting: Not a street scum or prison convict book. This is an up front, professional training manual featuring a conservative but effective military defense system with the flow and speed of Hapkido stick-fighting theory. Another Military Book Club selection, this book is a best-seller by an author who has dedicated a lifetime to the study and teaching of personal defense measures. $9.95

CHAPTER 12
THE IMPORTANCE
OF NETWORKING AND
GROUP FORMING

Say the word, "Survivalists", to most people and it engenders images of wild-eyed, machine gun toting red-necks in camo garb escaping to their mountain fortresses. This perception arose from the survivalist movement of the 1970's and 80's, which provided some justification in this view. Today, however, we know that survivalism, self-sufficiency, or self-reliance means different things than escape to a stronghold or fortress.

If you want to be able to ride out the tough times ahead, you need more than your own resources. You need the mutual support of like-minded folks who are willing to work together for the common cause of survival. Isolating oneself creates an inherent weakness. As Hemmingway said, "No man is an island." If someone wants to take you out, they can do so given time and opportunity. Protection by a group, however, means mutual protection. Each member brings unique and common skills and resources which, when pooled with others, create a much more complete

133

infrastructure for security and support.

Mothers can pool their talents and time to educate all the group's young. One family with an overabundance of grain may trade some for another family's excess beans. One family's work horse may plow several garden plots in return for bartered goods and services. If security watches must be established to protect vital resources, this responsibility may be shared by all so no one person is inordinately strapped.

The key is very few will be able to accumulate all the resources suggested in this book. But, within a large group, it may be possible to pool resources to gain an equivalent capability.

Start now to form relationships with others around you. Look to your church groups or your neighborhood. Even in large urban areas, it is possible to find others interested in forming mutual aid groups. Look at all the neighborhood crime-watch groups which have formed. This is a natural extension off of them.

Network with people from all over. Share information and ideas. The American Survival Guide has a section called the "Survivalist Directory". It serves as an interfacing agency for individuals and groups around the country and world who desire to network. The service is free and confidential.

If you form a group, determine the individual family necessities. Then create a list of resources which could be held in common. Perhaps a criteria for membership in such a group is for each family to agree to store the required necessities for itself and provide one major item which may be used by all. That way, one family might provide a roto-tiller, another a grain grinder, another a garden tractor, another a chainsaw, and so on.

Practice working together now, before times of stress happen. Create community garden plots and work rosters. Start now to work out personality differences and conflicts. Strive to attain a sense of teamship. Work together on projects such as the canning of fruits and vegetables. I can remember watching whole neighborhoods of Korean women working together to store Kimchi, a staple of their diet, for the winter. Large tarpaulins were spread in the street. On these were piled huge stacks of Chinese cabbages, onions, garlic, and red peppers. Each family brought their own ceramic kimchi storage jars. Ofttimes the piles of vegetables were twenty feet in diameter and five feet high.

The women worked together to wash, trim, shred, and otherwise prepare the ingredients. At the same time they chattered, sang songs, and joked with one another. They turned an onerous task which all would have had to do into a social occasion filled with happiness and sisterhood. I might add, it is these same social happenings which are the foundation for strong, mutually supporting relationships. This type of cooperation is very common in primitive societies where subsistence and communal survival depend on close relationships.

The important thing is to start now, get practiced, work out the bugs, and smooth out the operation before the challenging times come.

CHAPTER 13
SELF-SUFFICIENCY— A WAY OF LIFE

When I was a little boy, I thought everyone cooked on a wood/coal burning stove. I thought everyone had a cistern to catch rain water for clothes washing. A lockbox for us was not something one puts valuables into at the bank. It was where we put a steer at the locker plant after we butchered it and they cut and wrapped it.

Our chickens, which gave us eggs and Sunday dinner, ate bugs and weeds in the chicken yard and grain which we grew ourselves. The same went for our hogs, cattle, and our work horses before my grand dad transitioned to tractors. June/July was hay baling time. We put it in the hay mow over the barn and used it to feed the livestock (and to play in). My Grandfather's huge, work-hardened hands pulled on cow teats to obtain the milk we pasteurized for ourselves and for the others who bought it. He always remembered to shoot a few squirts into the yawning kittens' mouths as they meowed impatiently from the side of the milking stall.

In the Fall and Spring, he shoveled out the cow and horse barns and chicken house into our manure-spreader. These contents were spread over our fields and garden space to put nutrition back into the soil. His freshly plowed fields always produced endless amounts of nightcrawlers, which we used to feed the sun fish in Wild Cat Creek. They, in turn, fed us.

Everything was used and re-used. Little, if anything, was wasted. Cream was skimmed off the top of the milk and poured into a gallon jar. A special lid with paddles and a hand crank was screwed on and we made our own butter. There's nothing better than freshly made butter on biscuits hot out of the oven.

The fat and hide off a butchered pig was fried into scrapplings. Today these are made into a commercial product called pork rinds.

Our garden, which we called a truck patch, provided most of our vegetable and fruit needs. We had a grape arbor filled with concord grapes which made fantastic jelly stored in drinking glasses with paraffin wax seals.

One of the medicines we kept around the house was Alka-Seltzer. It came in tall, thin glass tubes. After we finished a tube, it became the mold for an emergency candle.

I didn't mean to bore you with all this nostalgia; however, it serves to describe our life on a self-sufficient farm. It really was a desirable lifestyle. We ate well and kept warm and dry in the winter. Our time was taken up with all kinds of useful activities. Most importantly, we lived well and honestly, beholden to no one. **Don't you think it's time to start seeking the same for yourself?**

Appendix A: Rotator Instructions

Did you ever make the mistake of not rotating cases of canned goods when you bought additional ones? Isn't it frustrating after a few months to discover case loads of bulged cans from spoilage because they weren't rotated properly? Many of us have probably made this mistake. This vertical storage canned goods automatic rotational system puts an end to unnecessary food spoilage and many stocking hassles.

MATERIEL LIST
FOR THE
CANNED GOODS AUTOMATIC
ROTATIONAL SYSTEM

a. 2 - 1" x 10" x 48" End Pieces

b. 1 - 1" x 10" x 46 1/2" Bottom Piece

c. 1 - 1" x 4" x 48" Front Plate

d. 1 - 4'x8' x 1/4" Masonite Sheet

e. 15 - 1"x48" Wooden Dowel Rods

f. Wood screws, wood glue, stain, paint, contact paper, etc.

Approximate cost of one 4' x 4' system = $65-$75. For a cheaper alternative, don't use dowels (by far the most expensive

element). Use a peg board cover in the front braced by internal framing. Plexiglass works well also.

INSTRUCTIONS
FOR BUILDING THE CANNED GOODS AUTOMATIC ROTATIONAL SYSTEM
(See the photos on page 142 and diagrams on page 148)

1. Saw the 4' x 8' sheet of masonite into two four foot square pieces. Saw one of the halfs into 16-6" x 48" strips. These will used for dividers between the rows of canned goods.

2. Draw a line the length of one end-piece the width of the cans you'll be storing plus an inch. It doesn't have to be exact. You'll find that a line about five inches from the edge will accomodate both three and four-inch diameter cans. Stack the two end-pieces together and drill a row of1-inch evenly spaced holes about 2' apart, centered on the drawn line per illustration #1. You'll find a C-clamp or two to be very helpful in holding the boards together exactly. Remember to hold the drill as straight up and down as possible.

3. Place one of the end pieces onto the stack of 6" x 48" masonite dividers. It's ok if the dividers don't touch the back of the rotational system so make sure there is enough space between the holes and the front edge of the dividers. Drill

Appendix A: Rotator Instructions

holes through them at each of the places drilled into the end-piece. A couple of C-clamps will again be helpful. Once you drill one hole through the stack, push one of the dowell rods through it to help keep the allignment of the dividers perfect. Next, drill a hole in the other end and use another dowell. Between these and the C-clamps, the stack should stay stable till all the holes are drilled.

4. Glue and screw the two end-pieces onto the ends of the bottom piece. Glue and screw the front plate onto the front of the end pieces and the bottom piece. Glue and screw the 4'x4' masonite sheet onto the back edge of the end pieces and bottom piece.

5. Thread the dowel rods through the end piece, through all dividers, and through the other end piece. If you are concerned with the appearance of the storage unit, sand and stain or paint the dowels and framework before doing this. Fasten optional end cover-pieces of masonite or contact paper once the dowels are in place. Leave the dividers free to slide back and forth on the dowels so various lengthed cans can easily be accomodated.

6. This unit is designed to be hung on a wall or set up on a shelf or overhang. It's possible to build taller units which go from floor to the ceiling if you don't mind reaching down to extract the canned goods. A good hanging mechanisim is two pieces of perforated metal strapping— one attached to each end of the back

piece. The easiest way to assure a level hang and the least ammount of mounting strain is to place a small table or a box against the wall area being covered. Set the rotational system on the table or box and mount it onto the wall. Remove the table or box.

7. Load from the top. The openings between the dowel rods allow you to see what is in each row and how much each needs to be replenished. The oldest purchase dates will always be on the bottom, ready for extraction from the row. No longer will you have to drag out cases of canned goods from a shelf so that the latest purchase can be stacked in the back.

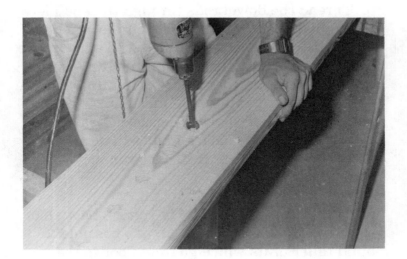

1. Drilling through the two end pieces.

Appendix A: Rotator Instructions

2. Aligning the stack of dividers under the end piece so there is enough room from the front edge to support the holes.

3. Threading a dowel rod through an end hole to help stabilize the stack.

4. A well-stabilized stack.

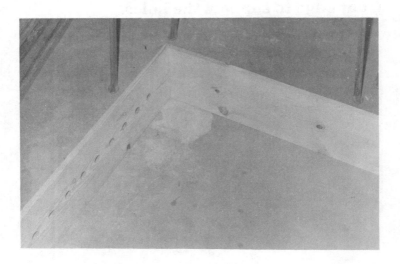

5. An end piece attached to the bottom piece.

Appendix A: Rotator Instructions

6. Attaching the front plate to the bottom piece.

7. Applying glue to the frame for the back piece.

Appendix A: Rotator Instructions

8. Assembling the dowel rods and dividers.
You may have to sweat and strain a little at
this step, getting the rods to line up with the
holes in the end pieces and the dividers.

9. Loading a can of peas from the top. It's
better to catch the can with one's fingers and
allow it to descend slowly a few rods at a time

than to simply drop a can like Candice is getting ready to do. It prevents significant can dents that way.

10. Cans stacked in the rotational system. Note, these mixed cans were for illustration purposes. In reality, only one type of product should be stacked per each row.

Appendix A: Rotator Instructions

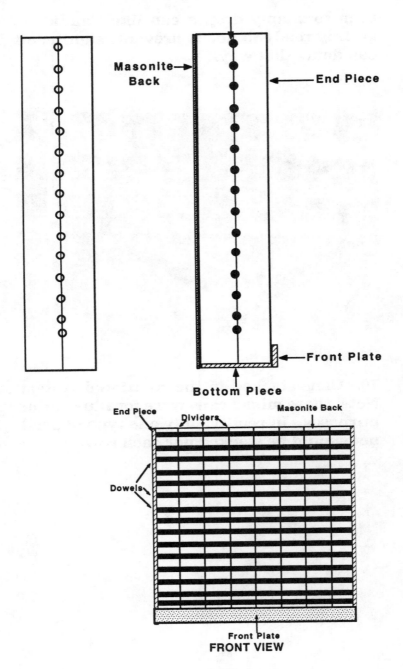

Masonite Back

End Piece

Front Plate

Bottom Piece

End Piece   Dividers   Masonite Back

Dowels

Front Plate
FRONT VIEW

148

UFD RESOURCE MAILORDER SECTION

Item #	Title	Price
1.	The New World Order:	$16.99
2.	En Route To Global Occupation:	$7.95
3.	The Aquarian Conspiracy:	$10.95
4.	The New Age Messiah:	$8.95
5.	Inside the New Age Nightmare:	$7.95
6.	En Route to Global Occupation:	$8.95
7.	Called to Serve:	$25.00
8.	The Blessings of Liberty:	$8.95
9.	Emergency Survival Packs:	$4.95.
10.	Emergency Preparedness Handbook:	$14.95.
11.	NITRO-PACK Catalog:	$3.00
12.	Reader's Digest Back to Basics	$26.00.
13.	Prepare Today— Survive Tomorrow:	$11.95.
14.	Skills for Survival:	$14.95.
15.	Survive Safely Anywhere:	$16.95.
16.	The Best of Woodsmoke :	$16.95.

Rodale Publishing/Yankee Magazine's Forgotten Arts Collection

17.	Forgotten Arts 1:	$6.95.
18.	Forgotten Arts 2:	$6.95.
19.	Forgotten Arts 3:	$6.95.
20.	Forgotten Arts 4:	$6.95.
21.	Forgotten Arts 5:	$6.95.
22.	Beginner's Guide to Family Preparedness :	$10.95.
23.	The New Seed Starters Handbook:	$14.95.
24.	Square Foot Gardening:	$14.95.
25.	Fool Proof Planting:	$14.95.

26. **Home Garden Hints**: $3.95.
27. **Rodale Book of Composting**: $14.95.
28. **Farmers of Forty Centuries** : $17.95.
29. **Saving Seeds**: $9.95.
30. **Rodale's All New Encyclopedia of Organic Gardening**: $29.95.
31. **Stocking Up III** : $24.95.
32. **The ABC's of Home Food Dehydration**: $7.95.
33. **Home Food Dehydrating**: $9.95.
34. **New Concepts In Dehydrated Food Cookery**: $12.95.
35. **Root Cellaring**: $12.95.
36. **The Home Water Source**: $16.96.
37. **Fun With Fruit Preservation** : $7.95.
38. **Cheese Making Made Easy**: $9.95.
39. **Jellies & Jams**: $6.95.
40. **Pickles & Relishes**: $6.95.
41. **Basic Butchering of Livestock and Game**: $11.95.
42. **Bee Prepared with Honey**: $9.95.
43. **Practical Beekeeping**: $9.95.
44. **Hive Management**: $14.95.
45. **Chickens in your Backyard**: $9.95.
46. **Ducks and Geese in your Backyard**: $9.95.
47. **Raising Poultry the Modern Way**: $9.95.
48. **Keeping Livestock Healthy**: $14.95.
49. **The Family Cow**: $12.95.
50. **Raising a Calf for Beef**: $7.95.
51. **Raising Milk Goats the Modern Way**: $9.95.
52. **Raising Sheep the Modern Way**: $9.95.
53. **Turning Wool into a Cottage Industry**: $14.95.

54. **Small Scale Pig Raising**: $12.95.
55. **A Veterinary Guide for Animal Owners**: $17.95.
56. **Laurel's Kitchen Bread Book**: $18.00.
57. **Doin' Dutch Oven Inside**: $8.95.
58. **Allied Cast Iron Cookware & Accessories Catalog**: $1.00.
59. **Dutch Oven Secrets**: $8.95.
60. **Lets Cook Dutch**: $7.95
61. **Dry Peas and Lentils**: $14.95.
62. **The Enchanted Broccoli Forest**: $16.95.
63. **Just Add Water**: $6.95.
64. **New Recipes From Moose Wood**: $13.95.
65. **Cooking Home Storage**: $12.95.
66. **Lehman's Non-Electric Catalog**: $2.00.
67. **Abundant Life Seeds Catalog**: $1.00.
68. **Native Seeds / Search**: $1.00
69. **Inside the New Age Nightmare**: $8.95.
70. **New Age Messiah Identified**: $9.95.
71. **The Big Book of Home Learning**: $69.00.
72. **From the Shepherd's Purse**: $26.00.
73. **The Healing Herbs**: $27.95.
74. **Rodale's Illustrated Encyclopedia of Herbs**: $24.95.
75. **The Doctor's Book of Home Remedies**: $26.95.
76. **Packing**: $11.95.
77. **Alternative Energy Sourcebook**: $16.00.
78. **Survival On The Battlefield— A Hand book to Military Martial Arts**: $14.95.
79. **Close Quarters Combat for Police and Security Forces**: $19.95
80. **Combination**: $30.00 special price.
81. **Surviving Hostage Situations**: $14.95.

82.   **Hapkido— The Integrated Fighting Art**: $12.95.
83.   **Military Knife Fighting**: $9.95.
84.   **Surviving Global Slavery**: $9.95.

To order, call 1-800-368-0877
or
Send to TREK-800, Dept UFD-NWO
P.O. Box I, Cave Junction, OR 97523

Shipping and Handling:

$3.00 for the first item. Add 50¢ for each item after that. UPS Ground will be the preferred shipping method and U.S. Book Rate postage the back-up means to ship. Allow 3-6 weeks for delivery. Allow a 3-week delay for personal checks.

INFORMATION SERVICE

Call our Self-Sufficiency information telephone for the latest tips on self-reliance. Call 1-900-287-2126 (99¢ per minute times 4 minutes).

UFD RESOURCE MAILORDER SECTION
(PHOTO COPY THIS PAGE)

ORDER BLANK

Item #	Title	Qty	Price
	Subtotal:		
	S&H:		
	Total:		

Name: _____

Address: _____

City, state, zip: _____

Check / Money Order Enclosed: _____

Credit Card Co. _____

Expiration Date: _____

Credit Card #: _____

Signature: _____

Send to: TREK-800, Dept UFD-NWO
P.O. Box "I", Cave Junction, OR 97523
or call 1-800-368-0877